Welcome

JACK FROST nipping at noses… merry carolers going from door to door…sugar cookies baking in the kitchen…they all mean one thing. It's Christmastime! And those special treats that come just once each year are all wrapped up here—in this newest edition of the holiday book for country-loving women.

From cover to cover, *Country Woman Christmas 2007* is packed with scrumptious seasonal recipes, handmade gifts and dazzling decorating ideas. You'll find 101 never-before-published holiday dishes, from impressive main courses and appetizers to festive desserts.

Dozens of easy-to-do Christmas craft projects are sure to get your creative juices flowing. And plenty of surprisingly simple how-to's for holiday decorating will make trimming your home delightful.

You'll also enjoy inspirational, true-life stories of Christmas miracles…seasonal poetry…a step-by-step guide for hosting a fun-filled holiday party…and much more.

So grab a cup of cocoa and curl up with *Country Woman Christmas 2007*. It'll make this holiday season your family's best yet!

44

10

Country Woman
Christmas
2007

ON THE COVER
Golden Santa Bread,
p. 72

112

74

18

104

62

Editor
Michelle Bretl

Art Director
Gretchen Trautman

Vice President, Executive Editor/Books
Heidi Reuter Lloyd

Senior Editor/Books
Mark Hagen

Layout Designer
Nancy Novak

Craft Editor
Jane Craig

Associate Editors
Jean Steiner, Sara Lancaster

Proofreader
Linne Bruskewitz

Editorial Assistant
Barb Czysz

Food Director
Diane Werner RD

Test Kitchen Manager
Karen Scales

Home Economists
Tina Johnson, Marie Parker, Annie Rose

Recipe Editors
Sue A. Jurack (Senior), Mary King,
Christine Rukavena

Recipe Asset System Manager
Coleen Martin

Contributing Copy Editor
Kris Krueger

Test Kitchen Assistant
Rita Krajcir

Studio Photographers
Rob Hagen (Senior), Dan Roberts,
Jim Wieland, Lori Foy

Senior Food Stylists
Sarah Thompson, Joylyn Trickel

Food Stylist Assistants
Kaitlyn Basasie, Alynna Malson

Set Stylists
Jennifer Bradley Vent (Senior),
Dee Dee Schaefer

Photo Studio Coordinator
Kathleen Swaney

Creative Director
Ardyth Cope

Senior Vice President, Editor in Chief
Catherine Cassidy

President
Barbara Newton

Founder
Roy Reiman

©2007 Reiman Media Group, Inc.
5400 S. 60th Street, Greendale WI 53129

International Standard Book Number (10):
0-89821-588-9
International Standard Book Number (13):
978-0-89821-588-5
International Standard Serial Number:
1093-6750

Share Your Holiday Joy

DO YOU celebrate Christmas in a special way? If so, we'd like to know! We're already gathering material for our next *Country Woman Christmas* book. And we need your help!

Do you have a nostalgic holiday story to share? Perhaps you've written a Yuletide poem or a fiction story.

Does your family carry on a favorite holiday tradition? Or do you deck your halls in some festive way? Maybe you know of a Christmas-loving country woman others might like to meet.

We'd also like *original* Christmas quilt patterns and craft projects, plus handmade gifts, decorations, etc. And don't forget to include your recipes for holiday main dishes, cookies, etc.

Send your ideas and photos to "CW Christmas Book," 5925 Country Lane, Greendale WI 53129. (Enclose a self-addressed stamped envelope if you'd like materials returned.) Or e-mail your ideas and photos to *bookeditors@reimanpub.com* (write "CW Christmas" on the subject line).

Christmas Decorating

This holiday season, deck your halls with the "do-it-yourself" ideas featured in this chapter. In no time, you'll make your Christmas extra bright.

Wonderful Wreaths

Spread holiday cheer all around with these festive wreath ideas, from a letter-perfect project to a silvery sensation.

Fruitful Greenery

(Pictured at left)

This bountiful wreath bursts with colorful dried papayas, tangelos, quinces, kiwano and other fruits to create a beautiful arrangement for Christmastime. Feel free to experiment with different fruits or to substitute more of the apples or pears.

MATERIALS NEEDED:
Three each medium tangelos, lemons, limes, kiwano and
    star fruit
Three each medium apples, papayas, pears and quinces
Lemon, orange or pineapple juice
15-inch oasis floral foam wreath frame
30 to 50 floral greening pins
Sheet moss to cover wreath frame
20 to 25 pine boughs, arborvitae and lemon leaf stems
    (6 inches each)
Two medium pomegranates, halved

Five kumquats or key limes, halved
One bunch Concord or seedless red grapes
Five medium pinecones
30 to 50 wired floral wood picks
Food dehydrator

DIRECTIONS:
In a dehydrator, dehydrate the citrus fruits, kiwano and star fruit according to manufacturer's directions until almost crisp. Cut apples, papayas, pears and quinces into 1/8- to 1/4-inch slices. Soak in lemon, orange or pineapple juice for 10-20 minutes. Drain and pat dry. Dehydrate. Store dried fruit in an airtight container.

Moisten sheet moss under running water; squeeze dry. Using greening pins, attach moss to all sides of the wreath frame.

Cut pine boughs, arborvitae and lemon leaf stems at an angle. Insert stems into sides and top of the foam frame. Attach halved fresh fruits, grape clusters, pinecones and dehydrated fruits using floral wood picks or greening pins.

C is for Christmas

(Pictured at right)

You'll spell out fun when you assemble this delightfully different accent. A decoupaged papier-mache "C" forms the "wreath," covered with purchased words that describe the holiday season.

MATERIALS NEEDED:
Papier-mache letter "C"
Green tissue paper
White craft glue
Water
Small container
1-inch foam brush
Scrapbook words of your choice
Red ribbon

DIRECTIONS:
Make a mixture of half white glue and half water.

Tear tissue paper into small squares. Use foam brush to apply glue mixture to a small area of the letter. Add a square of tissue and brush over it with more glue mixture.

Continue to add tissue paper in the same way, covering the front and sides of the letter. Let dry.

Glue scrapbook words to front of letter. Let dry.

Loop a length of ribbon around the top of the letter and tie the ends together to form a hanging loop.

Ornaments Galore

(Pictured on page 9)

With their vibrant colors and eye-catching shimmer, simple ball ornaments can create a stunning wreath for the holiday season. Choose a variety of wine and champagne hues as shown in the photo on page 9…or try experimenting with different color combinations, such as turquoise, green and silver.

MATERIALS NEEDED:

Wire wreath form and same-size circle of coordinating color stiff felt
Assorted colors and sizes of small ball ornaments with attached wires
Floral tape
Glue gun and glue stick
Craft wire
Wire cutters
Ruler
Scissors

DIRECTIONS:

Hold a group of five to seven ornaments in your hand, positioning the ornaments in a tight bunch. Twist all of the wires together to hold the ornaments in place.

Repeat with more ornaments to create enough bunches to cover the front and sides of the wire wreath form.

Wrap the twisted wires on each bunch of ball ornaments with floral tape.

Wire bunches of ball ornaments to the wire wreath form, positioning them as close as possible to each other and covering the entire front and sides of wire wreath form.

Glue the circle of felt to the back of wreath to help conceal the wire ends. Let dry.

Use scissors to cut out center of felt circle, cutting as close as possible to wire form.

For the hanging loop, use the wire cutters to cut a 6-inch length of craft wire.

Thread the 6-inch wire piece around the wire wreath form at the back of the wreath. Twist the ends of the wire piece together to form a hanging loop.

Snowflake Fantasy

(Pictured at left)

Wrap a long feather boa from the craft store around a plain foam wreath, and you'll have the foundation for this winter-white delight. Silvery sequins on pins fill the wreath with shiny snow crystals, and a metallic wire-edged ribbon tops it all off.

MATERIALS NEEDED:

Smooth white Styrofoam wreath form
White feather boa to cover wreath
Stick pins with silver ball heads
Silver snowflake sequins
Silver-lined bugle beads
3 yards of 1-1/2-inch-wide silver metallic wire-edged ribbon
Measuring tape
Scissors

DIRECTIONS:

Wrap the Styrofoam wreath form with the white feather boa, covering the wreath form completely. Pin the ends of the boa in place to hold it securely.

Place a silver snowflake sequin on a stick pin. Add one or two silver-lined bugle beads to the pin to prevent the sequin from falling into the boa. Insert the pin into the front of the wrapped Styrofoam wreath form where desired.

In the same way, add more sequins to the front of the wreath where desired.

For the ribbon hanger, cut a 24-inch length of silver metallic wire-edged ribbon. Loop the ribbon around the top of the wreath and tie the ribbon ends together. Use scissors to trim the ends.

Tie the remaining ribbon piece into a bow around the ribbon hanger on the wreath. Use scissors to trim the ends of bow as desired.

Victorian Decor Creates An Elegant Christmas

By Kathy DeLaney of
Jersey Shore, Pennsylva

THE SHIMMERING TREE and Santa-topped staircase in the foyer are among the first holiday sights to greet visitors at Kathy DeLaney's home. Beneath the tree, bright tins mimic 19th-century lithographs.

DURING the hustle and bustle of the holiday season, I welcome the chance to take a step back. And I *do* go back—all the way to the Victorian era!

I make this relaxing "retreat" every time I step into my Jersey Shore, Pennsylvania home, which I decorate completely in Victorian style for Christmas.

The 100-year-old house I share with my husband Donald, son Brandon and daughter Jenna has a Victorian feel year-round, with antique furnishings and bold wallpaper. In fact, moving here 11 years ago is what inspired my interest in 19th-century style.

But every Christmas, I take my old-fashioned decorating scheme even further. When I'm not working at a local bank, I'm often collecting Victorian Santas, dolls, tins and embroidered pillows to use as holiday accents.

Shades of burgundy, mauve, ivory and gold—popular decor colors during the reign of Queen Victoria—dominate in my house. You'll see very little of the bright red and green common in today's homes during December.

Elaborate Evergreen

The centerpiece of my holiday decor is the large Christmas tree in the foyer. Lacy angels, silky tassels, glass balls and other elegant ornaments hang from the tall tree. It's all wrapped up with ribbon and topped with another angel.

Antique-style tins and one of my favorite dolls sit on and around the lace skirt beneath. The tree is one of the first things guests see when they enter our home.

Nearby, the staircase showcases over half a dozen of my large Father Christmas figurines. They're dressed in all sorts of distinctive ways, from a patriotic suit to rustic ski gear.

For the finishing touch, I top off the banister with a bountiful garland of greenery and an antique candelabra.

Stately Sitting Room

Off of the foyer, the ornate hearth is the heart of the parlor. Candles, a long string of beads, family Christmas stockings, gauzy fabric and satin ribbon all brighten up the dark fireplace for the holiday season.

More of my Santa Claus figures surround the miniature tabletop Christmas tree in the center of the room. One thing's for sure—with all of these Christmasy faces around the house, I always feel like I have holiday guests!

Photos: Terry Wild

DECORATIVE DETAILS give Kathy's home the air of the Victorian period nearly everywhere you look. The needlepoint accent pillows and table runner in rich colors (above) call to mind traditional 19th-century embroidery. On the center table, a miniature tree is lushly covered with greens and floral trims.

Birds were a popular motif during the Victorian era, and the large white birdcage near the window adds to the 19th-century character.

With its antique furniture and formal appearance, my kids jokingly call the parlor our "museum." I admit that

(*Continued on next page*)

this room is more for looks than day-to-day living…but I love it all the same.

Taste of Christmas

In the dining room, another full-size Christmas tree hints at my passion for paper and lace Victorian fans. The romantic-looking tree features lacy fans that I created, as well as artificial roses, ribbon, glass ball ornaments, strings of beads and an angel topper.

You'll also spot a number of Christmas cards tucked among the branches. The tradition of exchanging greeting cards with friends and relatives during the holiday season became popular during the Victorian period.

On the dining table, my Christmas tablecloth adds another bold floral element to the room. That eye-catching pattern is offset by delicate contrasts, including the lacy photo holder displayed on the door.

All in all, the Victorian holiday accents that decorate my home during the Christmas season create a warm, festive and inviting feeling I really love. I wish I could leave them out year-round!

A FATHER CHRISTMAS from Kathy's sizable collection greets visitors near the front entrance to her home (top left), while both Mr. and Mrs. Claus have a cheery presence near the Christmas tree in the dining room (left). Another jolly old elf (below) relaxes next to a bench in the foyer, and a Victorian doll (inset) brings her charm to the main Christmas tree across the room.

SMALL BUT BIG on Victorian flair, a miniature tree trimmed with roses, beads and bows (above left) makes an eye-catching addition to the parlor. Another embellished tree, along with holiday towels and more of Kathy's Santa collection, enhances the antique washstand on the second floor (above right). Brightened by light from stained glass windows, the bold florals in the dining room (below) lend a romantic air to the Christmastime finery.

Display Your
Christmas Cards
In Creative Ways!

THE FLURRY of Christmas cards in our mailboxes each year has a way of filling our hearts with warmth and child-like anticipation. But after the cards are opened and read, you're left with the question: What am I going to do with them?

For many people, the tradition of displaying Christmas cards is almost as popular as sending them. Instead of throwing or packing away those holiday messages, they put out the cards for everyone to enjoy.

It sounds like a good idea, but how do you keep your mantels, windowsills and tabletops from looking cluttered? Easy! *Country Woman* Craft Editor Jane Craig has come up with four creative, space-saving ways to display your Christmas greetings throughout the holiday season.

You'll find that each of her delightful designs is simple to assemble. With a just a few materials and a little time, you can quickly transform ordinary items like a memo board, chicken wire, a wooden frame and ribbon into merry showcases.

Have a "Joyeux Noel" by trimming a plain French memo board for the holiday season. Embellishing the board with novelty buttons and festive braid gives it a touch of Christmas magic.

Or, try hanging your cards from bright ribbon attached to a greenery-trimmed window rod. It's a terrific solution when you don't have a lot of surface or wall space.

You'll see these and other festive displays on the next few pages. Just gather together your Christmas cards, then share their warmth with everyone who enters your home this holiday season.

French Flair

Trés belle…this beautiful card display starts with a French-style memo board from a craft store. Whether you stand the board on a table or hang it on a wall, this collection will add a European accent to your Yuletide decor.

How to do it: Remove the buttons on front of the purchased memo board, then glue red braid on top of the crisscrossing ribbons. (Make sure not to glue the braid to the fabric on the board.) When the braid is dry, glue coordinating Christmas novelty buttons where the original buttons had been. Your holiday cards will slip in neatly behind the decorated ribbons.

Grand Opening

Want to "make an entrance" at Christmastime? Try this dress-up idea for doors (shown at left). It's so simple, you'll have your holiday cards on display in mere moments.

How to do it: Wrap an entire door with wide Christmas ribbon as though you were wrapping a gift. Use the same ribbon and some thin wire to create a multi-loop bow and attach it to the door where the ribbon intersects. To add your cards, glue or staple them along the ribbon. Display all of your cards on a single door…or "wrap up" multiple doors and spread your cards throughout the house.

(Continued on next page)

Very Merry View

Get a fresh outlook on Christmas cards with this wonderful window treatment. The burst of color will make even the wintriest outdoor scene merry and bright.

How to do it: Drape a holly garland or other greenery over a curtain rod. Next, cut different lengths of narrow, red satin ribbon and tie one end of each piece to the curtain rod behind the garland. All that's left to do is glue or staple a Christmas card to the bottom end of each ribbon.

Country Collage

Chicken wire has never looked so cheery! A lifelong farm woman, *CW* Craft Editor Jane Craig decided to turn that rustic material into a fun and folksy showcase.

How to do it: After painting a stretcher frame, cut a piece of chicken wire to fit the back of the frame and staple the wire on. Miniature spring-type clothespins are the perfect homespun way to attach your cards. Finish with a raffia bow and any other decorations you like.

Instant Christmas

In mere minutes,
you can transform a
plain room into a
cheery Christmas
scene using common
household items.
Just try these
in-a-snap ideas!

DECORATING your home for
the holidays is a delightful way
to get into the Christmas spirit. It's a lot easier and less cost-
ly to do than you might think,
too! In this section, you'll see
how you can deck your halls using the ordinary, around-the-
house accents shown in the
dressed-up room at left.

Something as simple as placing red and green books on a
coffee table...filling dishes with
your extra ball ornaments...or
wrapping pictures on the wall
with holiday gift wrap...that's
all it takes. These ideas and
more will transform your rooms
from "everyday" to "Christmas
Day"—in an instant!

(Continued on next page)

Before

WHY KEEP your special holiday dishes hidden behind a cupboard door until Christmas dinner? Set them out on a coffee table or buffet for instant Yuletide decor all season long. Give empty mugs added fun with peppermint sticks or candy canes. Put unused Christmas tree ornaments, candles or narrow garlands inside bowls or on serving platters. The decorative ideas are endless!

MIXING AND MATCHING your on-hand accents will create an interesting, eclectic look. On this spirited window seat, red and clear glassware combine with ball ornaments and plain white pillar candles. Wrapping a plant pot with red florist's foil or fabric gives it seasonal flair in a flash.

SMALL TOUCHES can have a surprisingly big impact. Here, a leftover piece of beaded ribbon was hand-basted to the bottom inside edge of a plain lampshade. Suspended from the curtain rod with varying lengths of narrow ribbon, matching red ball ornaments make a simply striking focal point at the windows.

EXTRA GIFT WRAP is put to perfect use as a Christmasy covering for a painting above the fireplace. Around the wrapped-up art, a collection of candles, ceramics, bundled cinnamon sticks and more brings cheery variety to the hearth. Underneath those mantel accents, wide ribbon serves as a runner, anchored with unused tree ornaments at the ends.

TRIMMING this prelit artificial Christmas tree didn't take as long as it looks. The only added decoration is red ribbon! Pieces of it drape over the boughs gracefully in curls, and a multi-loop bow makes a matching topper. Near the tree, ribbon also enhances everyday accent pillows and ties back the curtains. With empty boxes and gift wrap, you can create a stack of presents for the base of the tree or any plain space.

Christmas Miracles

Chance encounters…lucky coincidences…unexpected blessings… read about these unforgettable events in the lives of country women.

Gift from an Angel

THE HOLIDAY SEASON was approaching, but I wasn't looking forward to it. The previous summer, my 48-year-old husband, Bill, died suddenly.

One evening, some friends and I decided to attend a local church supper and raffle of themed baskets. After the supper, we walked around the raffle tables, putting tickets in the baskets we liked best. I fell in love with one that had a favorite theme of mine—angels.

When the raffle started, we began to hear the winners announced. Over and over, names were called…but never ours. I found myself thinking, *Bill knew how much I love angels.*

Then came the angel basket. When the winner's name was read, I could hardly believe my ears. It was mine! I had a strange feeling as I walked up and claimed the pretty basket.

After one of my friends also won, we went back to my house to open the baskets and inspect the treasures inside. I opened mine, and the first thing I saw was an angel figurine holding a teddy bear.

Bill had collected antique bears…and had given them to me as gifts.

Looking at that angel and bear in her arms, I knew in my heart that Bill had given me another gift that Christmas.

~Ellen Baczek Amodeo, Derby, Connecticut

Dr. Santa Claus

WHEN I was 9 years old, my father became seriously ill. The doctor insisted that Dad not only quit his job, but also remain in bed for 2 months. We were forced to rely on the meager income Mom earned washing dishes.

At Christmastime, my parents broke the news to me that Santa wouldn't be coming that year. With a child's optimism, I thought, they must be wrong. Santa wouldn't forget me!

When Dad's health improved a bit, the doctor gave permission for a short outing on Christmas Eve. We visited friends, and I couldn't help feeling envious when I saw the beautiful gifts underneath their Christmas tree. I was sad to leave.

Then we got home—and stopped in our tracks outside the door. Piled high in front were at least a dozen gaily wrapped presents, some for all three of us. Mom and Dad were stunned. I had no doubt—they were from Santa!

Weeks later, we learned Santa's true identity. The doctor who'd been so concerned about my dad had provided the bounty of gifts. Not only that, he refused to accept payment for any of his home visits, medicine or other services.

And still to come was this generous doctor's most precious gift of all: a clean bill of health for my father.

~Kathy Holler, Andrew, Alberta

One Good Turn…

ON A COLD Christmas Day, I set out on snowy roads to have dinner at my sister's house. Halfway into the hour-long trip, I realized I'd forgotten to put gas in the car, and the tank was nearly empty.

I stopped at a nearby house and asked if any gas stations were open on the way to my sister's town. The homeowners said no but gave me enough of their own gas to get me there. When I tried to pay them, they refused, telling me to help someone else out instead.

A mile from my sister's house, a car was sitting on the roadside with a man and child inside. The man said they were out of gas, and he didn't want to take the child walking on the road. I was the only one who'd stopped to help.

I took them to the gas station in town, then filled my tank and finally arrived at my sister's, late for dinner. She gave me an earful about picking up a stranger!

When it was time to go, I started backing the car down the long driveway—and proceeded to slide right into the deep, snow-filled ditch. I sat there for a moment, stuck in the snow, frustrated and upset.

Just then, a car happened along and stopped. A man got out…and I saw it was the very same stranger I'd helped only a few hours ago! He got me out of the ditch and on my way home.

I still thank God for all of the miracles that happened on that Christmas. *~Nancy Landgraff, Henning, Minnesota*

Christmas Card Completed

I FIRST MET my future husband while we were working in Los Angeles aircraft factories during the early years of World War II. When he joined the Air Force and I went to the Womens Army Corps, we lost touch.

Both of our parents' homes were in Illinois, and in 1947 I received a Christmas card from him. In it, he wrote, "Please write to me." But when I looked at the envelope, I saw he had forgotten to include his return address!

I wrote to all three rural routes using the postmark. But, one by one, the letters all came back.

One night, there was a thunderstorm while we slept. A loud clap of thunder woke me up, and for some reason, a name—Roseville—was in my head. I went to look at a map. Sure enough—there was Roseville, a town near Macomb. I don't know why, but I was convinced: *That's where he is.*

I wrote one last letter, sent it off…and today, my husband and I give thanks every day for four children, six grandchildren and 12 great-grandchildren.

~Dorothy Anderson, Good Hope, Illinois

An angel of the Lord
appeared to them, and
the glory of the Lord
shone around them...

Luke 2:9

Stay, Christmas Tree

Dawn McCormick, Spring, Texas

Softly falls the winter darkness
While I sit beside this tree
Decked with ornaments, each giving
Me a special memory

Crocheted snowflakes, baby angels
Clothespin reindeer, wiggly-eyed
Lumpy wreaths of salt and flour
Golden horns with ribbons tied

Tiny lights of blue and scarlet
Sparkling in the quiet room
Standing tall this stately pine tree
Fills the air with its perfume

All too soon, I'll turn the lights off
Pack the ornaments away
Wrap the angel up in tissue
For another Christmas Day

So I sit here in the darkness
With my dreams of Christmas past
Lost in quiet reminiscence
Of the years that went too fast.

Snow Diamonds

Betsy Gilliland, Holton, Kansas

The golden moon shone brilliantly upon the icy path
Carefully I followed it, ignoring winter's wrath.

I gazed in speechless wonderment amidst an awesome sight:
Glistening and glimmering snow diamonds in the night.

Their beauty overwhelmed me as I stood and looked around
For millions winked and blinked at me from all across the ground.

These diamonds sparkled on the snow as far as eyes could see
And I was humbled at the riches God had shared with me.

Holiday Recipes

This special chapter has it all—from festive Christmas breakfasts to delectable desserts.

Pineapple Fruit Boat (p. 28)
Cherry Cider
Cheese 'n' Egg Pizza Squares

Best-Loved Brunch

With these hearty egg bakes, melt-in-your-mouth muffins, fresh fruit delights and more, you'll make Christmas morning as bright as can be.

Cheese 'n' Egg Pizza Squares

With an easy homemade crust, this family-pleasing pizza makes a delightfully different breakfast for Christmas. It's hard to stop at one slice! ~Janet Knickerbocker, Palmyra, Missouri

    1 package (1/4 ounce) active dry yeast
1-1/2 teaspoons sugar
1-1/4 cups warm water (110° to 115°)
1-1/4 teaspoons salt
    1 teaspoon nonfat dry milk powder
    3 cups all-purpose flour
    4 eggs, lightly beaten
    2 cups (8 ounces) shredded part-skim mozzarella
      cheese
    1 cup (4 ounces) shredded Muenster *or* Monterey
      Jack cheese
    2 tablespoons minced chives
  1/2 teaspoon garlic salt

1. In a large mixing bowl, dissolve yeast and sugar in warm water; let stand for 5 minutes. Add the salt, milk powder and 1-1/2 cups flour; mix well. Stir in enough remaining flour to form a soft dough. Do not knead.

2. Place in a greased bowl, turning once to grease top. Cover and let rise in a warm place until doubled, about 1 hour.

3. Punch dough down. Press into a greased 15-in. x 10-in. x 1-in. baking pan. Combine the eggs, cheese, chives and garlic salt; pour over crust. Bake at 350° for 20-25 minutes or until golden brown. Cut into squares. **Yield:** 10-12 servings.

Cherry Cider

This nicely spiced, simmered beverage is so warming. For a special holiday accent, garnish the mugs using maraschino cherries and a sliced orange. ~Marjorie Carey, Freeport, Florida

    4 cups apple cider
  3/4 cup orange juice
  1/4 cup maraschino cherry juice
    3 whole cloves
    3 whole allspice
    1 cinnamon stick
    1 orange peel strip (1 to 3 inches)
    6 maraschino cherries
    6 orange slices

1. In a large saucepan, combine the cider and juices. Place the cloves, allspice, cinnamon stick and orange peel on a double thickness of cheesecloth; bring up corners of cloth and tie with kitchen string to form a bag. Add to the pan.

2. Bring to a simmer over medium heat (do not boil). Simmer, uncovered, for 15 minutes. Discard spice bag. Serve cider warm in mugs; garnish with cherries and orange slices. **Yield:** 6 servings.

Sausage Mushroom Pie

A ready-to-bake pie shell speeds along the preparation of this delicious, hearty brunch dish. It's really satisfying during the cold winter months. ~Valerie Putsey, Winamac, Indiana

    1 pound bulk pork sausage
  1/4 cup chopped onion
    2 packages (10 ounces *each*) frozen chopped spinach,
      thawed and squeezed dry
    2 cans (8 ounces *each*) mushroom stems and pieces,
      drained
    2 eggs, lightly beaten
    3 cups (12 ounces) shredded part-skim mozzarella
      cheese
    1 unbaked deep-dish pastry shell (9 inches)
    1 cup (4 ounces) shredded cheddar cheese

1. In a large skillet, cook sausage and onion over medium heat until meat is no longer pink; drain. Stir in spinach and mushrooms. Combine the eggs and mozzarella cheese; fold into sausage mixture. Spoon into pastry shell.

2. Cover and bake at 400° for 30 minutes. Uncover; sprinkle with cheddar cheese. Bake 10-15 minutes longer or until cheese is melted. **Yield:** 6-8 servings.

Sausage Mushroom Pie

Mediterranean Frittata

Pineapple Fruit Boat

(Pictured on page 26)

Served in a pineapple shell, this fancy salad goes together surprisingly quickly with a handful of ingredients. It's an impressive way to present fresh fruit.   ~Nancy Reichert, Thomasville, Georgia

        1 fresh pineapple
    1-1/2 cups sliced fresh strawberries
        1 medium navel orange, peeled and sectioned
        1 medium firm banana, sliced
        2 ounces cream cheese, softened

1. Stand pineapple upright and vertically cut a third from one side, leaving the leaves attached; set cut piece aside.

2. Using a paring or grapefruit knife, remove the pineapple from the large section in strips, leaving a 1/2-in. shell; discard the core. Cut the strips into bite-size chunks. Set aside 2 tablespoons juice from the pineapple; invert the shell onto paper towel to drain.

3. Remove fruit from the small pineapple piece and cut into chunks; discard peel. Place shell in a large serving bowl or on a serving platter.

4. In a bowl, combine the pineapple chunks, strawberries, orange and banana. In a small mixing bowl, beat cream cheese and reserved pineapple juice; spoon over fruit and stir gently. Spoon into pineapple boat. Yield: 6 servings.

Make-Ahead Eggnog French Toast

My husband loves to try new recipes and discovered this eggnog-flavored toast. Preparing it the night before is a great time-saver for a busy morning.   ~Ann Marshall, Gladstone, Missouri

        5 slices white bread (1-1/4 inches thick)
        2 eggs
        2 cups eggnog
    1/2 teaspoon ground cinnamon
    1/2 teaspoon ground nutmeg
        4 tablespoons butter, melted, *divided*
Confectioners' sugar

1. Place the bread in an ungreased 13-in. x 9-in. x 2-in. baking dish. In a bowl, whisk the eggs, eggnog, cinnamon and nutmeg. Pour over bread. Cover and refrigerate for 8 hours or overnight.

2. Grease a 15-in. x 10-in. x 1-in. baking pan with 2 tablespoons melted butter. Carefully transfer bread to prepared pan. Brush with remaining butter.

3. Bake, uncovered, at 400° for 10 minutes. Carefully turn slices over. Bake 10-15 minutes longer or until golden brown and slightly puffed. Dust with confectioners' sugar. Serve immediately. Yield: 5 servings.

Editor's Note: This recipe was tested with commercially prepared eggnog.

Mediterranean Frittata

With red peppers, this delicious egg bake looks festive for Christmas. Italian bread, feta cheese and olives give the frittata Mediterranean flair.   ~Geraldine Evans, Hermosa, South Dakota

        2 medium onions, halved and thinly sliced
        2 garlic cloves, minced
        2 tablespoons olive oil
    1/2 cup chopped roasted sweet red peppers, drained
    1/2 cup chopped pimiento-stuffed olives
        3 cups cubed Italian bread
    1/2 cup crumbled feta cheese
        6 eggs
    1/2 cup chicken broth
    1/4 teaspoon pepper

1. In a large skillet, saute the onions and garlic in olive oil until tender. Remove from the heat. Stir in the sweet red peppers and olives. Place the Italian bread cubes in a greased 9-in. deep-dish pie plate. Top bread with the onion mixture and feta cheese.

2. In a bowl, whisk the eggs, broth and pepper; pour over cheese. Bake at 375° for 30-35 minutes or until a knife inserted near the center comes out clean. Let stand for 5 minutes before cutting into wedges. Yield: 6 servings.

Rum Raisin Muffins

Both men and women enjoy these rum-flavored, raisin-filled goodies. I think they're best served warm with mugs of hot coffee or cappuccino.   ~Lorraine Caland, Thunder Bay, Ontario

    1/2 cup butter, softened
    3/4 cup sugar
      2 eggs
      1 teaspoon rum extract
  1-1/2 cups plus 1 tablespoon all-purpose flour, *divided*
      2 teaspoons baking powder
    1/2 teaspoon baking soda
    1/3 cup milk
      1 cup raisins
    1/2 cup chopped pecans
    1/4 cup maple syrup

1. In a large mixing bowl, cream butter and sugar. Add eggs, one at a time, beating well after each addition. Beat in extract. Combine 1-1/2 cups flour, baking powder and baking soda; add to creamed mixture alternately with milk. Toss raisins with remaining flour. Fold raisins and pecans into batter.

2. Fill paper-lined muffin cups two-thirds full. Bake at 375° for 15-20 minutes or until a toothpick comes out clean. Immediately brush muffins with syrup. Cool for 5 minutes before removing from pans to wire racks. **Yield: 14 muffins.**

Country Pear Puff Pancake

This sweet, gooey pancake is dressed up with caramelized pears and baked until golden. Cut into serving-size wedges, it's a special change of pace.   ~Steffany Lohn, Brentwood, California

      5 tablespoons butter, *divided*
      3 medium pears, peeled and sliced
    1/2 cup packed brown sugar, *divided*
      1 tablespoon lemon juice
    1/2 cup all-purpose flour
    1/2 cup milk
      3 eggs, beaten
      2 tablespoons maple syrup
      1 teaspoon vanilla extract
    1/8 teaspoon salt
    1/2 teaspoon ground cinnamon
    1/4 teaspoon ground nutmeg

1. In a 10-in. ovenproof skillet over medium heat, melt 3 tablespoons butter. Add the sliced pears; cook and stir until tender, about 5 minutes. Stir in 1/4 cup brown sugar and the lemon juice.

2. In a bowl, whisk the flour, milk, eggs, syrup, vanilla and salt until smooth; pour over pears. Bake at 450° for 10-12 minutes or until puffy.

3. Meanwhile, in a microwave-safe bowl, melt remaining butter. Stir in the cinnamon, nutmeg and remaining brown sugar. Spread over pancake. Bake 8-10 minutes longer or until golden brown. Cut into wedges and serve immediately. **Yield: 4 servings.**

Upside-Down Apple Cake

Baked in a bundt pan and drizzled with icing, this breakfast cake will be a highlight of your holiday menu. I adapted the recipe from one of my grandmother's. ~Shaunda Wenger, Nibley, Utah

      2 egg whites
      1 cup sugar
      1 cup (8 ounces) sour cream
    1/2 cup unsweetened applesauce
      1 teaspoon vanilla extract
      2 cups all-purpose flour
      1 teaspoon baking powder
      1 teaspoon baking soda
    1/2 teaspoon salt
  FILLING:
  2-1/2 cups diced peeled tart apples
    1/2 cup chopped walnuts
    1/4 cup sugar
      2 tablespoons butter, melted
      2 teaspoons ground cinnamon
  GLAZE:
      1 cup confectioners' sugar
      4 teaspoons milk
    1/4 teaspoon vanilla extract

1. In a large mixing bowl, beat the egg whites, sugar, sour cream, applesauce and vanilla. Combine the flour, baking powder, baking soda and salt; gradually add to sour cream mixture, beating just until combined.

2. In a bowl, combine the filling ingredients. Spoon half of the batter into a greased and floured 10-in. fluted tube pan. Top with half of the filling. Repeat layers.

3. Bake at 350° for 40-45 minutes or until a toothpick inserted near the center comes out clean. Cool for 10 minutes; invert pan and remove cake to a wire rack to cool completely. Combine glaze ingredients; drizzle over cake. **Yield: 14 servings.**

Upside-Down Apple Cake

Cinnamon-Glazed Butterhorns

and place point side down 2 in. apart on greased baking sheets. Curve ends to form a crescent.

4. Cover and let rise in a warm place until doubled, about 30 minutes. Bake at 350° for 12-15 minutes or until golden brown. Remove from pans to wire racks.

5. For glaze, heat butter in a small saucepan until golden brown; remove from the heat. In a bowl, whisk the confectioners' sugar, cinnamon, vanilla and browned butter until smooth. Whisk in enough hot water to achieve spreading consistency. Brush over warm rolls. **Yield:** 2 dozen.

Chocolate Pecan Waffles

Topped with fresh strawberries and chocolate whipped cream, these tender breakfast treats are rich and luscious enough to be served as dessert. They're sure to delight your family on Christmas morning. ~Diane Halferty, Corpus Christi, Texas

   3/4 cup semisweet chocolate chips
   3/4 cup butter, cubed
     2 cups all-purpose flour
   1/2 cup sugar
     3 teaspoons baking powder
   3/4 teaspoon salt
     3 eggs
 1-1/2 cups milk
     3 teaspoons vanilla extract
   1/2 cup chopped pecans, toasted
Chocolate whipped cream in a can and sliced fresh
   strawberries, optional

1. In a microwave-safe bowl, melt chocolate chips and butter; stir until smooth. Cool to room temperature.

2. In a large bowl, combine the flour, sugar, baking powder and salt. In another bowl, whisk the eggs, milk and vanilla; stir into dry ingredients until smooth. Stir in pecans and chocolate mixture (batter will be thick).

3. Bake in a preheated waffle iron according to manufacturer's directions. Garnish with whipped cream and strawberries if desired. **Yield:** 20 waffles.

Cinnamon-Glazed Butterhorns

I cook for a logging crew, and these golden goodies are always a hit. I used to spread them with canned frosting, but then I came up with an easy glaze. ~Susan Zacharias, La Crete, Alberta

     1 package (1/4 ounce) active dry yeast
   1/4 cup warm water (110° to 115°)
     1 cup warm milk (110° to 115°)
   1/2 cup butter, melted
   1/4 cup sugar
     1 egg
   3/4 teaspoon salt
     4 to 4-1/4 cups all-purpose flour
GLAZE:
     3 tablespoons butter
     1 cup confectioners' sugar
   3/4 teaspoon ground cinnamon
     1 teaspoon vanilla extract
     1 to 2 tablespoons hot water

1. In a large mixing bowl, dissolve yeast in warm water. Add the milk, butter, sugar, egg, salt and 2 cups flour; beat until smooth. Add enough remaining flour to form a soft dough.

2. Turn onto a floured surface; knead until smooth and elastic, about 6-8 minutes. Place in a greased bowl, turning once to grease top. Cover and let rise in a warm place until doubled, about 1 hour.

3. Punch dough down. Turn onto a lightly floured surface; divide in half. Roll each portion into a 12-in. circle; cut each circle into 12 wedges. Roll up wedges from the wide end

Cran-Orange Fruit Dip

Tart, sweet and nutty flavors all blend together beautifully in this quick-to-fix, chunky fruit dip. I like it best with slices of apples and pears. ~Cheryl Miller, Fort Collins, Colorado

     1 cup (8 ounces) vanilla yogurt
   1/2 cup chopped pecans
   1/2 cup cranberry-orange sauce
   1/2 teaspoon ground cinnamon
   1/4 teaspoon ground nutmeg
Assorted fresh fruit

In a bowl, combine the first five ingredients. Cover and refrigerate for at least 1 hour. Serve with fruit. Refrigerate leftovers. **Yield:** 1-1/3 cups.

Cran-Orange Fruit Dip
Chocolate Pecan Waffles

Czech Christmas Bread (p. 35)
Butterscotch Bubble Bread

Bountiful Breads

Christmas just isn't the same without golden brown loaves, tempting coffee cakes, home-style rolls and other fresh-baked favorites.

Butterscotch Bubble Bread

This is a "must-have" treat in our house at holiday time. Baked in a tube pan, the delectable loaf is chock-full of cherries, nuts and coconut. ~Jacki Lesandrini, Crystal Falls, Michigan

  16 maraschino cherries, drained and patted dry
  1/3 cup chopped nuts
  1/3 cup flaked coconut
   1 loaf (1 pound) frozen bread dough, thawed and cut
     into 24 pieces *or* 24 frozen bread dough dinner
     rolls, thawed
   1 package (3-1/2 ounces) cook-and-serve
     butterscotch pudding mix
  1/4 cup packed brown sugar
  1/2 teaspoon ground cinnamon
   6 tablespoons butter, melted

1. Arrange cherries on the bottom of a greased 10-in. fluted tube pan. Sprinkle with nuts and coconut. Arrange dough pieces over coconut.

2. Combine the pudding mix, brown sugar and cinnamon; sprinkle over dough. Drizzle with butter. Cover and let rise in a warm place until doubled, about 1-1/2 hours.

3. Bake at 375° for 20-25 minutes or until golden brown. Cool for 5 minutes before inverting onto a serving plate. Serve warm. Yield: 12-14 servings.

Pecan Sticky Buns

These homemade caramel rolls have the old-fashioned goodness my family craves. Tender and nutty, the buns disappear fast on Christmas. ~Julia Spence, New Braunfels, Texas

   4 to 4-1/2 cups all-purpose flour
  1/3 cup sugar
   1 package (1/4 ounce) active dry yeast
  1/2 teaspoon salt
   1 cup milk
  1/4 cup butter
   2 eggs
TOPPING:
  1/3 cup butter
  2/3 cup packed brown sugar
   2 tablespoons light corn syrup
   1 cup chopped pecans
FILLING:
   3 tablespoons butter, melted
  1/2 cup packed brown sugar
  1/3 cup sugar
   2 tablespoons ground cinnamon

1. In a large mixing bowl, combine 2 cups flour, sugar, yeast and salt. In a small saucepan, heat milk and butter to 120°-130°. Add to dry ingredients; beat just until moistened. Add eggs; beat until smooth. Stir in enough remaining flour to form a soft dough (dough will be sticky).

2. Turn onto a floured surface; knead until smooth and elastic, about 6-8 minutes. Place in a greased bowl, turning once to grease top. Cover and let rise in a warm place until doubled, about 1 hour.

3. For topping, in a small saucepan, melt butter over medium heat. Stir in brown sugar and corn syrup until combined. Pour into a well-greased 13-in. x 9-in. x 2-in. baking dish. Sprinkle with pecans.

4. Punch dough down. Turn onto a floured surface. Roll into a 12-in. x 8-in. rectangle; brush with melted butter. Combine sugars and cinnamon; sprinkle over dough to within 1/2 in. of edges and press into dough. Roll up jelly-roll style, starting with a long side; pinch seam to seal.

5. Cut into 12 slices. Place cut side down in prepared pan. Cover and let rise until doubled, about 30 minutes. Bake at 375° for 20-25 minutes or until golden brown. Immediately invert onto a serving platter. Serve warm. Yield: 1 dozen.

Pecan Sticky Buns

Cinnamon Doughnut Twists

square, make two 1-in. vertical cuts 1/2 in. apart. Braid the three attached strips; pinch ends to seal. Place on a greased baking sheet. Repeat with remaining squares and the remaining dough.

4. Cover and let rise until almost doubled, about 40 minutes. In an electric skillet or deep-fat fryer, heat oil to 375°. Fry doughnuts, a few at a time, for 1 minute on each side or until golden brown. Remove with a slotted spoon to paper towels.

5. In a large saucepan, combine glaze ingredients. Bring to a rolling boil over medium heat. Remove from the heat. Dip warm doughnuts in glaze. Place on wire racks with waxed paper underneath. **Yield: 6 dozen.**

Danish Raisin Ring

This is an old-fashioned recipe updated for the bread machine. Loaded with raisins and pecans, the nicely spiced coffee cake is scrumptious.   ~Esther Danielson, Lake Arrowhead, California

    1 cup water (70° to 80°)
    6 tablespoons butter, softened
    1 egg
    1 teaspoon salt
  1/3 cup nonfat dry milk powder
    6 tablespoons sugar
1-1/4 teaspoons ground cardamom
3-1/4 cups bread flour
    1 package (1/4 ounce) active dry yeast
FILLING:
  3/4 cup chopped pecans
  3/4 cup golden raisins
  1/2 cup raisins
  1/4 cup sugar
    1 teaspoon ground cinnamon
GLAZE (optional):
1-1/2 cups confectioners' sugar
    2 to 3 tablespoons milk
  1/4 teaspoon vanilla extract

1. In bread machine pan, place the first nine ingredients in order suggested by manufacturer. Select dough setting (check dough after 5 minutes of mixing; add 1 to 2 tablespoons of water or flour if needed).

2. When cycle is completed, turn dough onto a lightly floured surface. Knead in pecans and raisins. Roll into a 14-in. x 9-in. rectangle. Combine sugar and cinnamon; sprinkle over dough to within 1/2 in. of edges.

3. Roll up jelly-roll style, starting with a long side; pinch seam to seal. Place seam side down in a greased 10-in. fluted tube pan. Pinch ends together to form a ring. Cover and let rise in a warm place until doubled, about 40 minutes.

4. Bake at 375° for 30-35 minutes or until golden brown. Cool for 10 minutes before removing from pan to a wire rack. If desired, combine glaze ingredients and drizzle over the top. **Yield: 1 coffee cake.**

Editor's Note: If your bread machine has a time-delay feature, we recommend you do not use it for this recipe.

Cinnamon Doughnut Twists

These melt-in-your-mouth, glazed goodies were adapted from a South African recipe. I make them at Christmastime, and they never last long.   ~Peggy Boudreau, Bridgewater, Nova Scotia

    1 package (1/4 ounce) active dry yeast
  1/4 cup warm water (110° to 115°)
    1 cup warm milk (110° to 115°)
  1/2 cup butter, softened
  1/3 cup packed brown sugar
    1 teaspoon sugar
    1 teaspoon ground nutmeg
  1/2 teaspoon salt
    2 eggs, beaten
    2 teaspoons grated orange peel
    5 cups all-purpose flour
Oil for deep-fat frying
GLAZE:
1-1/2 cups sugar
    1 cup water
  1/2 teaspoon ground cinnamon

1. In a large mixing bowl, dissolve yeast in warm water. Add milk, butter, sugars, nutmeg, salt, eggs and orange peel; mix well. Beat in 2 cups flour. Beat on medium speed for 3 minutes or until smooth. Stir in enough remaining flour to form a firm dough.

2. Turn onto a floured surface; knead until smooth and elastic, about 6-8 minutes. Place in a greased bowl, turning once to grease top. Cover and let rise in a warm place until doubled, about 45 minutes.

3. Punch dough down. Divide in half. On a floured surface, roll out one portion into a 13-1/2-in. x 6-in. rectangle. With a sharp knife, cut dough into thirty-six 1-1/2-in. squares. Using a sharp knife and beginning at the bottom of the lower left

Czech Christmas Bread

(Pictured on page 32)

My grandmother and aunt used to bake these lovely, traditional loaves every Christmas. I like my slice toasted and buttered for breakfast. ~Donna Lamb, Marseilles, Illinois

2 packages (1/4 ounce *each*) active dry yeast
1/2 cup warm water (110° to 115°)
3/4 cup sugar
3/4 cup warm milk (110° to 115°)
1/2 cup butter, softened
2 eggs
1 tablespoon grated lemon peel
1 teaspoon salt
1/4 teaspoon ground mace
5-1/2 to 6 cups all-purpose flour
3/4 cup golden raisins
1 egg yolk
1 tablespoon water

1. In a large mixing bowl, dissolve yeast in warm water. Add the sugar, milk, butter, eggs, lemon peel, salt, mace and 3 cups flour. Beat on medium speed for 2 minutes or until smooth. Stir in enough remaining flour to form a soft dough (dough will be sticky).

2. Turn onto a lightly floured surface; knead until smooth and elastic, about 6-8 minutes. Place in a greased bowl, turning once to grease top. Cover and let rise in a warm place until doubled, about 1 hour.

3. Punch dough down. Turn onto a lightly floured surface; knead in raisins. Divide dough into six equal portions. Shape each into a 20-in. rope. Place three ropes on a greased baking sheet; braid. Pinch ends to seal and tuck under. Repeat with remaining ropes.

4. Cover and let rise in a warm place until doubled, about 45 minutes. Beat egg yolk and water; brush over loaves. Bake at 350° for 25-30 minutes or until golden brown. Cool on wire racks. **Yield:** 2 loaves.

Scandinavian Rye Crisps

To celebrate our Norwegian heritage, my family's Christmas feast includes many Scandinavian dishes. These crispy little rounds made with rye flour are one of the "can't-miss" specialties on our holiday menu. ~Gloria Bisek, Deerwood, Minnesota

1-1/2 cups all-purpose flour
1 cup rye flour
2 tablespoons brown sugar
2 teaspoons caraway seeds
1 teaspoon baking powder
1/2 teaspoon salt
1/4 cup cold butter
1/2 cup water

1. In a large bowl, combine the first six ingredients; cut in butter until mixture resembles coarse crumbs. Gradually add water, tossing with a fork until dough forms a ball (dough will be dry).

2. Turn onto a floured surface; knead 10 times. Divide dough into 10 pieces. Roll each piece into a 6-in. circle. Place on greased baking sheets. Prick entire surface of each circle with a fork.

3. Bake at 325° for 12-15 minutes or until firm. Turn; bake 6-7 minutes or until edges are lightly browned. Remove to wire racks to cool. **Yield:** 10 crisps.

Sweet Potato Rolls

This recipe uses a convenient bread machine to create a batch of home-style rolls. They're wonderful served warm with honey and butter. ~Peggy Burdick, Burlington, Michigan

1/2 cup water (70° to 80°)
1 egg
3 tablespoons butter, softened
3/4 cup mashed sweet potatoes (without added milk *or* butter)
4 to 4-1/2 cups all-purpose flour
3 tablespoons sugar
1-1/2 teaspoons salt
2 packages (1/4 ounce *each*) active dry yeast

1. In bread machine pan, place all ingredients in order suggested by manufacturer. Select dough setting (check dough after 5 minutes of mixing; add 1 to 2 tablespoons of water or flour if needed).

2. When cycle is completed, turn dough onto a lightly floured surface. Punch down. Divide into 30 portions; roll each into a ball. Place on greased baking sheets. Cover and let rise in a warm place until doubled, about 30 minutes. Bake at 400° for 8-10 minutes or until golden brown. Serve warm. **Yield:** 2-1/2 dozen.

Editor's Note: If your bread machine has a time-delay feature, we recommend you do not use it for this recipe.

Sweet Potato Rolls

White Chocolate Cranberry Muffins

White Chocolate Cranberry Muffins

I wasn't sure how these muffins would go over with my family, but everyone raved about the combination of white chocolate and dried cranberries.   ~Erica Keip, Cambria, Wisconsin

    2 cups all-purpose flour
    1 cup sugar
    2 teaspoons baking powder
    1/2 teaspoon salt
    2 eggs
1-1/3 cups buttermilk
    1/2 cup butter, melted
    1 cup dried cranberries
    2 squares (1 ounce *each*) white baking chocolate, grated
    1/2 cup confectioners' sugar
    4 to 5 teaspoons cranberry juice

1. In a large bowl, combine the flour, sugar, baking powder and salt. In another bowl, whisk the eggs, buttermilk and butter. Stir into dry ingredients just until moistened. Fold in cranberries and chocolate.

2. Fill greased or paper-lined muffin cups two-thirds full. Bake at 400° for 15-18 minutes or until a toothpick comes out clean. Cool for 5 minutes before removing from pans to wire racks to cool completely.

3. In a small bowl, combine confectioners' sugar and cranberry juice until smooth. Drizzle over muffins. **Yield:** 15 muffins.

Tomato Spinach Bread

I've been making these savory swirled loaves for many years. The red and green colors really add to the festive feel of Christmas dinner.   ~Avanell Hewitt, North Richland Hills, Texas

    1 package (1/4 ounce) active dry yeast
    1 cup warm water (110° to 115°)
    4 teaspoons butter, melted
    1 teaspoon salt
2-3/4 to 3 cups bread flour
SPINACH DOUGH:
    1/4 cup cold water
    1 package (10 ounces) frozen chopped spinach, thawed and squeezed dry
    1 package (1/4 ounce) active dry yeast
    3/4 cup warm water (110° to 115°)
    4 teaspoons butter, melted
    1 teaspoon salt
3-1/4 to 3-1/2 cups bread flour
TOMATO DOUGH:
    1 package (1/4 ounce) active dry yeast
    1 cup warm water (110° to 115°)
    4 teaspoons butter, melted
    1 teaspoon salt
    1 can (6 ounces) tomato paste
3-1/4 to 3-3/4 cups bread flour
    1 egg white
    1 teaspoon cold water

1. For plain dough, in a large mixing bowl, dissolve yeast in warm water. Add butter, salt and 2 cups flour; beat until smooth. Add enough remaining flour to form a firm dough. Turn onto a lightly floured surface; knead until smooth and elastic, about 6-8 minutes. Place in a greased bowl, turning once to grease top. Cover and refrigerate overnight.

2. For spinach dough, puree cold water and spinach in a food processor. In a large mixing bowl, dissolve yeast in warm water. Add butter, salt, 2 cups flour and spinach mixture; beat until smooth. Add enough remaining flour to form a firm dough. Turn onto a lightly floured surface. With lightly floured hands, knead until smooth and elastic, about 6-8 minutes. Place in a greased bowl, turning once to grease top. Cover and refrigerate overnight.

3. For tomato dough, in a large mixing bowl, dissolve yeast in warm water. Add butter, salt, tomato paste and 2 cups flour; beat until smooth. Add enough remaining flour to form a firm dough. Turn onto a lightly floured surface. With lightly floured hands, knead until smooth and elastic, about 6-8 minutes. Place in a greased bowl, turning once to grease top. Cover and refrigerate overnight.

4. Punch down each dough and divide in half; cover. On a lightly floured surface, roll out one portion of each dough into a 10-in. x 8-in. rectangle. Place a rectangle of spinach dough on plain dough; top with tomato dough. Roll into a 12-in. x 10-in. rectangle. Roll up jelly-roll style, starting with a long side; pinch seams to seal and tuck ends under. Place seam side down on a greased baking sheet. Repeat with remaining dough.

5. Cover loaves and let rise in a warm place until doubled, about 30 minutes. With a sharp knife, make three shallow diagonal slashes across the top of each loaf. Beat egg white and cold water; brush over loaves. Bake at 350° for 35-45 minutes or until golden brown. Remove to wire racks to cool. **Yield:** 2 loaves.

Tomato Spinach Bread

No-Yeast Stollen

No-Yeast Stollen

We always knew it was Christmas when my mother-in-law sent us a German stollen. Now, our grown children continue to have stollen for the holidays. My daughter-in-law shared this recipe that doesn't use yeast. ~Marjorie Mueller, Mariposa, California

2 tablespoons chopped candied orange peel
2 tablespoons chopped candied lemon peel
4 teaspoons water
1 teaspoon rum extract
1/4 teaspoon almond extract
1/4 teaspoon vanilla extract
2-1/2 cups all-purpose flour
3/4 cup sugar
1/2 cup ground almonds
2 teaspoons baking powder
1/2 teaspoon salt
1/4 teaspoon ground mace
1/8 teaspoon ground cardamom
5 tablespoons cold butter, *divided*
1 cup small-curd cottage cheese
2 eggs, beaten
1/2 cup golden raisins
1/2 cup dried currants
2 teaspoons confectioners' sugar

1. In a small bowl, combine the candied peel, water and extracts; set aside. In a large bowl, combine the flour, sugar, almonds, baking powder, salt, mace and cardamom. Cut in 4 tablespoons butter until mixture resembles fine crumbs.

2. Stir in the cottage cheese, eggs, raisins, currants and candied peel mixture; form into a ball. Turn onto a floured surface; knead five times. Roll dough into a 10-in. x 8-in. oval. Fold a long side over to within 1 in. of opposite side; press edge lightly to seal.

3. Place on a greased baking sheet; curve ends slightly. Melt remaining butter; brush over dough. Bake at 350° for 45-50 minutes or until golden brown. Cool on a wire rack. Dust with confectioners' sugar. **Yield:** 1 loaf.

Glazed Walnut-Lemon Loaf

Moist and tender, this beautiful loaf looks and tastes like a cross between bread and pound cake. Cooled slices are excellent for tea sandwiches. ~Adelaide Muldoon, Springfield, Virginia

6 tablespoons shortening
1-1/3 cups sugar, *divided*
2 eggs
1 tablespoon grated lemon peel
1-1/2 cups all-purpose flour
1 teaspoon baking powder
1/2 teaspoon salt
1/2 cup milk
1/2 cup chopped walnuts
3 tablespoons lemon juice

1. In a large mixing bowl, cream shortening and 1 cup sugar. Add eggs, one at a time, beating well after each addition. Beat in lemon peel. Combine the flour, baking powder and salt; add to creamed mixture alternately with milk. Fold in walnuts.

2. Pour into a greased and floured 9-in. x 5-in. x 3-in. loaf pan. Bake at 350° for 45-50 minutes or until a toothpick inserted near the center comes out clean. Cool for 10 minutes.

3. In a small bowl, whisk lemon juice and remaining sugar until sugar is dissolved; pour over bread. Cool 10 minutes longer; remove from pan to a wire rack to cool completely. **Yield:** 1 loaf.

Currant Hazelnut Scones

With an ever-expanding dairy farm and three children, I don't have a lot of time to bake. But when I can, I pull out this recipe for sweet scones. ~Jill Boettcher, Mayer, Minnesota

2 cups all-purpose flour
1/2 cup sugar
2 teaspoons baking powder
1/3 cup cold butter
2 eggs
1/4 cup milk
1/2 cup chopped hazelnuts, toasted
1/2 cup dried currants

1. In a large bowl, combine the flour, sugar and baking powder. Cut in butter until mixture resembles coarse crumbs. In a small bowl, whisk eggs and milk; stir into crumb mixture just until moistened. Fold in hazelnuts and currants (dough will be sticky).

2. Turn onto a floured surface; knead 10 times. Pat into an 8-in. circle. Cut into eight wedges. Separate wedges and place on a greased baking sheet. Bake at 375° for 12-18 minutes or until golden brown. Serve warm. **Yield:** 8 scones.

Apple-Nut Quick Bread

Every year when the apples are ready for picking, my husband says, "How about making a loaf of that apple bread?" This recipe featuring pecans came from a friend and has received many blue ribbons. ~Lorraine Retzlaff, Shawano, Wisconsin

3 cups all-purpose flour
1 teaspoon baking soda
1 teaspoon baking powder
1-1/8 teaspoons ground cinnamon, *divided*
1/2 teaspoon salt
2 eggs
1-1/2 cups plus 2 tablespoons sugar, *divided*
1 cup vegetable oil
3 cups chopped peeled tart apples
1 cup chopped pecans

1. In a large bowl, combine the flour, baking soda, baking powder, 1 teaspoon cinnamon and salt. In a small mixing bowl, beat the eggs, 1-1/2 cups sugar and oil. Stir in apples; let stand for 5 minutes. Stir into dry ingredients just until moistened. Fold in pecans.

2. Pour into two greased and floured 8-in. x 4-in. x 2-in. loaf pans. Combine remaining sugar and cinnamon; sprinkle over batter. Bake at 350° for 50-60 minutes or until a toothpick inserted near the center comes out clean. Cool for 10 minutes before removing from pans to wire racks. **Yield:** 2 loaves.

Lemon Bran Muffins

Bran cereal lends heartiness to these lemon-poppy seed muffins. For a sweet-tangy finishing touch, drizzle on the confectioners' sugar glaze. ~Rosalea Hoeft, Kimball, Minnesota

2 cups All-Bran
1-1/4 cups milk
1 egg
3 tablespoons vegetable oil
1 tablespoon lemon juice
1-1/4 cups all-purpose flour
2/3 cup sugar
3 teaspoons baking powder
1/2 teaspoon salt
1 tablespoon poppy seeds
2 teaspoons grated lemon peel
GLAZE:
3/4 cup confectioners' sugar
3 to 4 teaspoons lemon juice

1. In a large bowl, combine bran and milk; let stand for 5 minutes. Stir in the egg, oil and lemon juice. Combine the flour, sugar, baking powder and salt; stir into bran mixture just until moistened. Fold in poppy seeds and lemon peel.

2. Fill greased or paper-lined muffin cups two-thirds full. Bake at 400° for 18-22 minutes or until a toothpick comes out with moist crumbs. Cool for 5 minutes before removing from pan to a wire rack. Combine the glaze ingredients; drizzle over warm muffins. **Yield:** 1 dozen.

Swirled Pumpkin Yeast Bread

I call this my "hostess gift" pumpkin bread, but it's fantastic for any occasion at all. Swirls of cinnamon-sugar make every slice irresistible. ~Shirley Runkle, St. Paris, Ohio

4-1/2 to 5 cups all-purpose flour
3 cups whole wheat flour
2 cups quick-cooking oats
2/3 cup packed brown sugar
2-1/2 teaspoons pumpkin pie spice
1-1/2 teaspoons salt
1 teaspoon sugar
2 packages (1/4 ounce *each*) active dry yeast
1-1/2 cups warm water (120° to 130°)
1/3 cup vegetable oil
1 cup canned pumpkin
1/3 cup unsweetened applesauce
2 eggs, lightly beaten
1/2 cup raisins
FILLING:
1/4 cup butter, softened
1/2 cup packed brown sugar
1 teaspoon ground cinnamon

1. In a large mixing bowl, combine 2 cups all-purpose flour, whole wheat flour, oats, brown sugar, pumpkin pie spice, salt, sugar and yeast. Beat in warm water, oil, pumpkin and applesauce just until moistened. Add eggs; beat until smooth. Stir in enough remaining all-purpose flour to form a firm dough. Add raisins.

2. Turn onto a lightly floured surface; knead until smooth and elastic, about 6-8 minutes. Place in a greased bowl, turning once to grease top. Cover and let rise in a warm place until doubled, about 1 hour.

3. Punch dough down. Turn onto a lightly floured surface; divide in half. Roll each portion into an 18-in. x 9-in. rectangle; brush with butter to within 1/2 in. of edges. Combine brown sugar and cinnamon; sprinkle over dough. Roll up jelly-roll style, starting with a short side; pinch seam to seal.

4. Place seam side down in two greased 9-in. x 5-in. x 3-in. loaf pans. Cover; let rise until doubled, about 30 minutes. Bake at 350° for 55-65 minutes or until golden brown. Cool for 10 minutes before removing from pans to wire racks. **Yield:** 2 loaves.

Swirled Pumpkin Yeast Bread

Pesto Cheese Blossom
Almond-Bacon Cheese Crostini (p. 42)
Prosciutto Phyllo Roll-Ups (p. 42)

Elegant Appetizers

★ *For every festive get-together during the holiday season, rely on the wide variety of impressive hors d'oeuvres and seasonal snacks here.* ★

Pesto Cheese Blossom

With colorful layers, this pretty spread is a real attention-getter at holiday gatherings. I like the convenience of making it ahead of time. ~Mary Lou Timpson, Colorado City, Arizona

        9 slices provolone cheese, *divided*
    1/3 cup oil-packed sun-dried tomatoes
CREAM CHEESE LAYER:
        2 packages (8 ounces *each*) cream cheese, cubed
    1/2 cup pistachios
        2 garlic cloves, peeled
PESTO LAYER:
    1/2 cup pine nuts
    1/2 cup packed fresh basil leaves
    1/2 cup packed fresh parsley sprigs
    1/4 teaspoon salt
    1/4 teaspoon pepper
        1 tablespoon olive oil
Assorted crackers

1. Line a 1-qt. bowl with plastic wrap, overlapping the sides of the bowl. Arrange six cheese slices on the bottom and up the sides of the bowl, overlapping each slice; set aside.

2. Drain tomatoes, reserving 3 teaspoons oil mixture. In a food processor, combine tomatoes and reserved oil mixture; cover and process until blended. Transfer to a small bowl; set aside.

3. Place cream cheese, pistachios and garlic in the food processor; cover and process until blended. Transfer to a small bowl; set aside.

4. Add the pine nuts, basil, parsley, salt and pepper to food processor; cover and process until blended. While processing, add oil; process for 15 seconds or until combined. Transfer to a small bowl.

5. Spread a third of the cream cheese mixture over provolone cheese in prepared bowl. Layer with pesto mixture, another third of the cream cheese mixture, tomato mixture and remaining cream cheese mixture. Top with remaining provolone slices.

6. Bring edges of plastic wrap together over cheese; press down gently to seal. Refrigerate for at least 4 hours or until firm. Open plastic wrap; invert mold onto a serving plate. Serve with crackers. **Yield:** 24 servings.

Honey Nut Spread

This simple cream cheese treat goes over big at all my ladies' luncheons and parties. No one guesses that the spread has just four ingredients. ~Sheryl Jennings, Clarksdale, Mississippi

        1 package (8 ounces) cream cheese, softened
    1/4 cup sour cream
        2 tablespoons honey
    1/4 cup chopped pecans
Gingersnap cookies

In a small mixing bowl, beat the cream cheese, sour cream and honey until well blended; stir in pecans. Cover and refrigerate for at least 1 hour. Serve with gingersnaps. **Yield:** 1-1/2 cups.

Eggcellent Finger Sandwiches

Tartar sauce gives these little egg salad sandwiches a slightly sweet flavor. Cut into bell shapes with olive "clappers," they look festive for Christmas. ~Vikki Rebholz, West Chester, Ohio

        4 hard-cooked eggs, chopped
        5 bacon strips, cooked and crumbled
    1/4 cup tartar sauce
      16 slices swirled rye and pumpernickel bread
        2 tablespoons butter, softened
      16 slices pimiento-stuffed olives, optional

1. In a small bowl, combine the eggs, bacon and tartar sauce. Cover and refrigerate for 30 minutes.

2. Using a 2-1/2-in. bell-shaped cookie cutter, cut out two bells from each slice of bread. Lightly spread one side of each bell with butter. Spread egg mixture over half of buttered bells; top with remaining bells, buttered side down.

3. If desired, garnish each sandwich with an olive slice, securing with a small amount of egg mixture. Cover and refrigerate until serving. **Yield:** 16 sandwiches.

Eggcellent Finger Sandwiches

Curried Chicken Cream Puffs

I've made these fluffy puffs for baby showers as well as holiday parties. The savory bites have such a nice mixture of lightness and crunch. ~Kerry Vaughn, Kalispell, Montana

      1/2 cup water
      1/3 cup butter, cubed
   Dash salt
      1/2 cup all-purpose flour
         2 eggs
   FILLING:
         1 package (8 ounces) cream cheese, softened
      1/4 cup milk
      1/4 teaspoon salt
      1/4 teaspoon curry powder
   Dash pepper
    1-1/2 cups cubed cooked chicken
      1/3 cup slivered almonds, toasted
         1 green onion, chopped

1. In a large saucepan, bring water, butter and salt to a boil. Add flour all at once and stir until a smooth ball forms. Remove from the heat; let stand for 5 minutes. Add eggs, one at a time, beating well after each addition. Continue beating until mixture is smooth and shiny.

2. Drop by rounded teaspoonfuls 2 in. apart onto greased baking sheets. Bake at 425° for 15-20 minutes or until golden brown. Remove to wire racks. Immediately split puffs open; remove tops and set aside. Reduce heat to 375°.

3. In a small mixing bowl, beat the cream cheese, milk, salt, curry powder and pepper until smooth. Stir in the chicken, almonds and onion. Spoon into puffs; replace tops. Place on a baking sheet; bake for 5 minutes or until heated through. Yield: 2 dozen.

Prosciutto Phyllo Roll-Ups

(Pictured on page 40)

These elegant finger foods use delicate phyllo dough. With artichoke sauce on the side, the cheesy rolls make extra-special hors d'oeuvres. ~Michaela Rosenthal, Woodland Hills, California

      24 sheets phyllo dough (14 inches x 9 inches)
      1/4 cup butter, melted
         8 thin slices prosciutto, cut into 1-inch strips
      24 fresh asparagus spears, trimmed
      24 fresh green beans, trimmed
   ARTICHOKE SAUCE:
      1/4 cup sour cream
      1/2 teaspoon lemon juice
         1 jar (6 ounces) marinated artichoke hearts, drained
         2 ounces cream cheese, softened
      1/4 cup chopped roasted sweet red peppers, drained
         3 tablespoons grated Parmesan cheese
         2 green onions, chopped
         1 garlic clove, peeled
      1/4 teaspoon white pepper
      1/4 teaspoon cayenne pepper

1. Line baking sheets with parchment paper; set aside. Place one sheet of phyllo dough on a work surface (keep remaining dough covered with plastic wrap and a damp towel to avoid drying out). Brush with butter; fold in half lengthwise. Brush with butter; fold in half widthwise.

2. Brush with butter; top with a prosciutto strip. Place an asparagus spear and a green bean at a diagonal on bottom right corner; roll up. Repeat with remaining dough, butter, prosciutto and vegetables.

3. Place roll-ups on prepared sheets. Bake at 400° for 6-8 minutes or until golden brown. Meanwhile, in a blender, combine sauce ingredients. Cover; process until smooth. Transfer to a bowl; serve with roll-ups. Yield: 2 dozen (1 cup sauce).

Almond-Bacon Cheese Crostini

(Pictured on page 40)

For a change from the usual toasted tomato appetizer, try these baked bites. If you like, slice the baguette at an angle instead of making a straight cut. ~Leondre Hermann, Stuart, Florida

         1 French bread baguette (1 pound), cut into 36 slices
         2 cups (8 ounces) shredded Monterey Jack cheese
      2/3 cup mayonnaise
      1/2 cup sliced almonds, toasted
         6 bacon strips, cooked and crumbled
         1 green onion, chopped
   Dash salt
   Additional toasted almonds, optional

1. Place bread slices on an ungreased baking sheet. Bake at 400° for 8-9 minutes or until lightly browned.

2. Meanwhile, in a bowl, combine the cheese, mayonnaise, almonds, bacon, onion and salt. Spread over bread. Bake for 7 minutes or until cheese is melted. Sprinkle with additional almonds if desired. Serve warm. Yield: 3 dozen.

Beef Con Queso Dip

This meaty snack really hits the spot on chilly days. It's a tradition to serve the dip with tortilla chips, but I also like it with homemade soft pretzels. ~Wendy Weaver, Leetonia, Ohio

- 1 pound ground beef
- 3/4 cup chopped onion
- 1/2 cup chopped green pepper
- 1 pound process cheese (Velveeta), cubed
- 1 can (8 ounces) tomato sauce
- 1 can (4 ounces) chopped green chilies
- 1 tablespoon brown sugar
- 1 tablespoon Worcestershire sauce
- 1-1/2 teaspoons paprika
- 3/4 teaspoon cayenne pepper
- 1/2 teaspoon salt

Tortilla chips

In a large skillet, cook the beef, onion and green pepper over medium heat until meat is no longer pink; drain. Stir in the cheese, tomato sauce, chilies, brown sugar, Worcestershire sauce, paprika, cayenne and salt. Cook and stir until cheese is melted. Serve warm with tortilla chips. **Yield:** 4 cups.

Hot Mushroom Tidbits

You can't miss with tried-and-true appetizers like this one. In fact, I've been relying on these yummy biscuit bites for more than 20 years. ~Beverly Zdurne, East Lansing, Michigan

- 1 package (3 ounces) cream cheese, softened
- 1 can (4 ounces) mushroom stems and pieces, drained and chopped
- 2 tablespoons diced pimientos
- 1 tablespoon chopped onion
- 2 drops hot pepper sauce
- 1 tube (12 ounces) refrigerated flaky buttermilk biscuits
- 1/3 cup salad croutons, crushed

1. In a small bowl, combine the cream cheese, mushrooms, pimientos, onion and hot pepper sauce. Separate dough into 10 biscuits; roll each into a 4-in. circle. Spread each with a heaping teaspoonful of mushroom mixture. Roll up and seal edges. Cut each into four slices; roll in crouton crumbs.

2. Place on ungreased baking sheets. Bake at 375° for 12-14 minutes or until golden brown. Serve warm. Refrigerate leftovers. **Yield:** 40 appetizers.

Creamy Olive-Bacon Dip

When I had just 15 minutes to prepare something for a party, I combined the ingredients I had on hand and came up with this cheesy dip. I knew the recipe was a keeper when I took home a nearly empty bowl. ~Kari Caven, Post Falls, Idaho

- 1 cup (8 ounces) sour cream
- 12 bacon strips, cooked and crumbled
- 3/4 cup mayonnaise
- 3/4 cup shredded cheddar cheese
- 2 cans (2-1/4 ounces *each*) sliced ripe olives, drained
- 1 medium tomato, seeded and chopped

Bagel chips *or* assorted crackers

In a bowl, combine the first six ingredients. Refrigerate until serving. Serve with bagel chips or crackers. **Yield:** 3 cups.

Sweet 'n' Sour Appetizer Meatballs

Since a friend shared this recipe with me several years ago, I've fixed it many times. The tangy meatballs also make a great main dish served with potatoes. ~Lucretia Burt, Tallassee, Alabama

- 1 egg
- 1/2 cup quick-cooking oats
- 1 envelope onion soup mix
- 2 pounds ground beef
- 2 cans (5-1/2 ounces *each*) apricot nectar
- 3/4 cup packed brown sugar
- 3/4 cup ketchup
- 1/3 cup cider vinegar
- 2 tablespoons prepared mustard
- 1 tablespoon prepared horseradish

Minced fresh parsley

1. In a large bowl, combine the egg, oats and soup mix. Crumble beef over mixture and mix well. Shape into 1-in. balls.

2. Place 1 in. apart on a greased rack in a 15-in. x 10-in. x 1-in. baking pan. Bake at 400° for 18-20 minutes or until no longer pink. Drain on paper towels.

3. In a large skillet, combine the apricot nectar, brown sugar, ketchup, vinegar, mustard and horseradish. Bring to a boil. Reduce heat; simmer, uncovered, for 10 minutes. Add meatballs; simmer 15 minutes longer or until heated through. Sprinkle with parsley. **Yield:** 4 dozen.

Sweet 'n' Sour Appetizer Meatballs

Walnut-Cranberry Lattice Pie (p. 46)
Barded Turkey with Corn Bread Stuffing

Dazzling Dinners

★ *On Christmas Day, gather loved ones around an unforgettable feast featuring any of these memorable main courses and accompaniments.* ★

Barded Turkey with Corn Bread Stuffing

As a newlywed, I didn't know much about roasting a turkey. Then our pastor, an excellent cook, told me about barding—placing or tying bacon on the turkey to prevent drying during roasting. The fat bastes the turkey while it cooks, keeping it moist and adding flavor. ~Anita Briner, Etters, Pennsylvania

```
    3/4 pound bulk pork sausage
      1 medium red onion, chopped
      1 package (16 ounces) corn bread stuffing
      2 medium apples, peeled and chopped
      1 cup raisins
    1/2 cup butter, melted
      1 to 2 tablespoons poultry seasoning
    1/2 teaspoon crushed red pepper flakes
2-1/2 to 3 cups chicken broth
      1 turkey (16 pounds)
      1 pound sliced bacon, divided
```

1. In a large skillet, cook sausage and onion until meat is no longer pink; drain. Transfer to a large bowl; add the stuffing, apples, raisins, butter, poultry seasoning and pepper flakes. Add broth; toss to combine.

2. Just before baking, loosely stuff turkey. Skewer turkey openings; tie drumsticks together. Place breast side up on a rack in a roasting pan. Place several bacon strips over the turkey.

3. Bake, uncovered, at 325° for 1 hour; replace bacon with new bacon strips (discard cooked bacon or save for another use). Bake 3-1/2 to 4 hours longer or until a meat thermometer reads 180° for the turkey and 165° for the stuffing, replacing bacon each hour and basting occasionally with pan drippings. (Cover loosely with foil if turkey browns too quickly.)

4. Cover turkey and let stand for 20 minutes before removing stuffing and carving. Remove bacon strips before serving. **Yield:** 16 servings (12 cups stuffing).

Editor's Note: Stuffing may be prepared as directed and baked separately in a greased 3-qt. baking dish. Cover and bake at 325° for 40 minutes. Uncover and bake 10 minutes longer or until lightly browned.

Harvest Squash Medley

To me, cooking is an art, and I love trying new recipes. This one dresses up baked butternut squash, sweet potatoes and apples with citrus and spices. ~Ruth Cowley, Pipe Creek, Texas

```
      6 cups water
      1 butternut squash, peeled, seeded and cut into
        3/4-inch pieces
      2 medium sweet potatoes, peeled and cut into
        3/4-inch pieces
    1/4 cup honey
    1/4 cup orange juice
      3 tablespoons butter
      1 tablespoon grated orange peel
    1/2 teaspoon ground cinnamon
    1/8 teaspoon ground nutmeg
      2 small apples, peeled and sliced
    1/2 cup chopped walnuts, toasted
```

1. In a large saucepan, bring water to a boil. Add squash and return to a boil. Reduce heat; cover and simmer for 10 minutes. Drain. Place squash and sweet potatoes in a greased 13-in. x 9-in. x 2-in. baking dish.

2. In a small saucepan, combine the honey, orange juice, butter, orange peel, cinnamon and nutmeg. Bring to a boil, stirring constantly. Pour over squash and potatoes.

3. Cover and bake at 350° for 30 minutes, stirring occasionally. Uncover; stir in apples. Bake 30-35 minutes longer or until tender, stirring occasionally. Sprinkle with walnuts. **Yield:** 10 servings.

Harvest Squash Medley

Traditional Lasagna

Traditional Lasagna

For a casual holiday meal, you can't go wrong with this rich and meaty lasagna. My grown sons and daughter-in-law request it for their birthdays, too. ~Pam Thompson, Girard, Illinois

        9 lasagna noodles
1-1/4 pounds bulk Italian sausage
    3/4 pound ground beef
        1 medium onion, diced
        3 garlic cloves, minced
        2 cans (one 28 ounces, one 15 ounces) crushed
            tomatoes
        2 cans (6 ounces *each*) tomato paste
    2/3 cup water
        2 to 3 tablespoons sugar
        3 tablespoons plus 1/4 cup minced fresh parsley,
            divided
        2 teaspoons dried basil
    3/4 teaspoon fennel seed
    3/4 teaspoon salt, *divided*
    1/4 teaspoon coarsely ground pepper
        1 egg, beaten
        1 carton (15 ounces) ricotta cheese
        4 cups (16 ounces) shredded part-skim mozzarella
            cheese
    3/4 cup grated Parmesan cheese

1. Cook noodles according to package directions. Meanwhile, in a large saucepan or Dutch oven, cook the sausage, beef, onion and garlic over medium heat until meat is no longer pink; drain.

2. Stir in the tomatoes, tomato paste, water, sugar, 3 tablespoons parsley, basil, fennel seed, 1/2 teaspoon salt and pepper. Bring to a boil. Reduce heat; simmer, uncovered, for 30 minutes, stirring occasionally. In a small bowl, combine the egg, ricotta, and remaining parsley and salt.

3. Drain noodles. Spread 2 cups meat sauce into an ungreased 13-in. x 9-in. x 2-in. baking dish. Layer with three noodles and a third of the ricotta mixture. Sprinkle with 1 cup mozzarella and 2 tablespoons Parmesan. Repeat layers twice. Top with remaining meat sauce and cheeses.

4. Cover and bake at 375° for 25 minutes. Uncover; bake 25 minutes longer or until bubbly. Let stand for 15 minutes before cutting. **Yield: 12 servings.**

Walnut-Cranberry Lattice Pie

(Pictured on page 44)

After this ruby-red pie got rave reviews on Thanksgiving, I was happy to bake it again for Christmas dinner. The naturally tart cranberries are perfectly sweetened and accented with walnuts, raisins and lemon. ~Shirley Glaab, Hattiesburg, Mississippi

Pastry for double-crust pie (9 inches)
        1 tablespoon cornstarch
    1/4 cup water
    3/4 cup sugar
    3/4 cup light corn syrup
        1 teaspoon grated lemon peel
        1 package (12 ounces) fresh *or* frozen cranberries
    1/2 cup raisins
    1/2 cup chopped walnuts
        2 tablespoons butter

1. Line a 9-in. pie plate with the bottom pie pastry; trim to 1 in. beyond the edge of the pie plate. Set remaining pastry aside for top of pie.

2. In a large saucepan, combine cornstarch and water until smooth. Stir in the sugar, corn syrup and lemon peel; bring to a boil over medium heat. Add cranberries and raisins; cook and stir for 4-6 minutes or until the berries pop. Remove from the heat; stir in walnuts and butter. Pour into crust.

3. Roll out remaining pastry; make a lattice crust. Seal and flute edges. Bake at 425° for 30-40 minutes or until filling is bubbly and crust is golden brown. Cool on a wire rack. **Yield: 6-8 servings.**

Marinated Broccoli-Cauliflower Salad

My mother made this for a family gathering several years ago, and I've been serving it ever since. Everyone enjoys this well-dressed salad. ~Kathy Jacques, Chesterfield, Michigan

        1 small bunch broccoli, cut into florets
        1 small head cauliflower, broken into florets
    1/2 pound sliced fresh mushrooms
        1 small red onion, halved and sliced

1/2 cup vegetable oil
1/4 cup sugar
  2 tablespoons cider vinegar
3/4 teaspoon onion salt
1/2 teaspoon paprika

In a large bowl, combine the broccoli, cauliflower, mushrooms and onion. In a jar with a tight-fitting lid, combine the remaining ingredients; shake until sugar is dissolved. Pour over vegetables and toss gently to coat. Cover and refrigerate overnight, stirring occasionally. **Yield:** 10 servings.

Tarragon Potatoes

These cubed, unpeeled red potatoes make an attractive side dish for any Christmas feast. Tarragon, onion and garlic give them terrific flavor. ~Marjorie Sours, Tiffin, Ohio

  2 teaspoons chicken bouillon granules
1/2 cup boiling water
  2 tablespoons white vinegar
  2 tablespoons olive oil
  1 tablespoon minced fresh tarragon *or* 1 teaspoon dried tarragon
  2 garlic cloves, minced
1/4 teaspoon pepper
  2 pounds small red potatoes, quartered
  1 small onion, chopped

1. In a small bowl, dissolve bouillon in water. Stir in the vinegar, oil, tarragon, garlic and pepper. Place the potatoes in a greased 11-in. x 7-in. x 2-in. baking dish. Add tarragon mixture and stir to coat. Sprinkle with onion.

2. Bake, uncovered, at 350° for 1-1/4 to 1-1/2 hours or until tender. **Yield:** 8 servings.

Crisp Cranberry Gelatin

How can gelatin be "crisp?" When it's chock-full of chopped apple and celery! This tangy favorite gets a nice crunch from walnuts, too. ~Janet Statham, Spartanburg, South Carolina

  2 cups fresh *or* frozen cranberries
1-1/2 cups water
  1 cup sugar
  1 package (3 ounces) orange gelatin
  1 medium apple, chopped
  1 celery rib, chopped
1/2 cup chopped walnuts
1/4 cup orange juice
  2 teaspoons grated orange peel

1. In a large saucepan, bring cranberries and water to a boil. Reduce heat; simmer for 3 minutes or until the berries pop, stirring occasionally. Stir in sugar and gelatin until dissolved. Pour into an 11-in. x 7-in. x 2-in. dish; refrigerate until set but not firm, about 1 hour.

2. Combine the apple, celery, walnuts, orange juice and peel; stir into the gelatin mixture. Refrigerate until firm. **Yield:** 12 servings.

White Chocolate-Strawberry Tiramisu

This decadent dessert is a twist on traditional Italian tiramisu. My family loves the unusual addition of white chocolate and fresh strawberries. ~Anna Ginsberg, Austin, Texas

  2 cups heavy whipping cream
  1 package (8 ounces) cream cheese, softened
  4 ounces Mascarpone cheese
  9 squares (1 ounce *each*) white baking chocolate, melted and cooled
  1 cup confectioners' sugar, *divided*
  1 teaspoon vanilla extract
  2 packages (3 ounces *each*) ladyfingers, split
2/3 cup orange juice
  4 cups sliced fresh strawberries
Chocolate syrup, optional

1. In a large mixing bowl, beat cream until soft peaks form; set aside. In another large mixing bowl, beat cheeses until light and fluffy. Beat in the chocolate, 1/2 cup confectioners' sugar and vanilla. Fold in 2 cups whipped cream.

2. Brush half of the ladyfingers with half of the orange juice; arrange in a 13-in. x 9-in. x 2-in. dish. Spread with 2 cups cream cheese mixture; top with 2 cups of berries. Brush remaining ladyfingers with remaining orange juice; arrange over the berries.

3. Combine remaining cream cheese mixture and confectioners' sugar; fold in remaining whipped cream. Spread over ladyfingers. Top with remaining berries. Refrigerate until serving. Just before serving, drizzle with chocolate syrup if desired. Refrigerate leftovers. **Yield:** 15 servings.

White Chocolate-Strawberry Tiramisu

Cheddar Corn Chowder

Cheddar Corn Chowder

My children absolutely love this rich, zippy soup. They have just one complaint—it seems I never make a big enough batch to suit them! ~Marlene Leschinsky, Winnipeg, Manitoba

    1 medium onion, chopped
    1 cup diced sweet red pepper, *divided*
    2 tablespoons butter
1/4 cup all-purpose flour
    2 cups chicken *or* vegetable broth
    2 large potatoes, diced
    1 can (11 ounces) whole kernel corn, drained
       or 1-1/2 cups frozen corn
1/2 teaspoon ground mustard
1/2 teaspoon paprika
1/4 teaspoon salt
1/4 teaspoon crushed red pepper flakes
1/8 teaspoon pepper
    2 cups milk
1-1/2 cups (6 ounces) shredded cheddar cheese
    4 green onions, thinly sliced

1. In a large saucepan, saute onion and 1/2 cup red pepper in butter until tender. Stir in flour until blended; gradually add broth. Bring to a boil; cook and stir for 1 minute or until thickened.

2. Add the potatoes, corn, mustard, paprika, salt, pepper flakes and pepper; return to a boil. Reduce heat; cover and simmer for 15-20 minutes or until potatoes are tender.

3. Add milk and remaining red pepper; cook and stir until soup comes to a boil. Remove from the heat; stir in cheese until melted. Sprinkle with green onions. **Yield:** 8 servings (2 quarts).

Apple Cider-Glazed Ham

When I wanted to try something new with our holiday ham, I created this cider glaze. It's slightly sweet but still has the spicy flavor my family craves. ~Rebecca LaWare, Hilton, New York

1/2 fully cooked bone-in ham (6 to 7 pounds)
    2 cups apple cider
    1 cup honey
1/2 cup cider vinegar
1/4 cup Dijon mustard
    1 tablespoon butter
    2 teaspoons chili powder
1/2 teaspoon apple pie spice

1. Place ham on a rack in a shallow roasting pan. Score the surface of the ham, making diamond shapes 1/2 in. deep. Cover and bake at 325° for 2 hours.

2. Meanwhile, in a saucepan, combine the apple cider, honey, cider vinegar and mustard; bring to a boil. Reduce heat; simmer, uncovered, for 15 minutes, stirring frequently. Stir in the butter, chili powder and apple pie spice. Set aside 1 cup of sauce for serving.

3. Cook the remaining sauce until thickened; spoon over ham. Bake, uncovered, 30-35 minutes longer or until a meat thermometer reads 140°. Warm reserved sauce; serve with ham. **Yield:** 10 servings (1 cup sauce).

Comforting Cranberry-Apple Crisp

The first time I baked this bubbly, golden brown crisp, I knew it was a winner. Cranberry sauce adds the perfect amount of tartness to every spoonful. ~Kara Cook, Elk Ridge, Utah

3/4 cup sugar
    2 tablespoons all-purpose flour
    1 can (16 ounces) whole-berry cranberry sauce
    7 cups thinly sliced peeled tart apples
TOPPING:
    1 cup old-fashioned oats
1/3 cup all-purpose flour
1/3 cup packed brown sugar
1/4 cup chopped walnuts
    1 teaspoon ground cinnamon
1/4 cup cold butter
Vanilla ice cream, optional

1. In a large bowl, combine sugar and flour; stir in cranberry sauce. Add apples; toss to coat. Transfer to a greased 13-in. x 9-in. x 2-in. baking dish.

2. For the topping, in a small bowl, combine the oats, flour, brown sugar, walnuts and cinnamon; cut in the butter until the mixture resembles coarse crumbs. Sprinkle the topping over apple mixture.

3. Bake at 375° for 35-40 minutes or until filling is bubbly and topping is golden brown. Serve warm with ice cream if desired. **Yield:** 12-15 servings.

Cheddar Corn Chowder
Buttery Almond Green Beans (p. 50)
Apple Cider-Glazed Ham
Comforting Cranberry-Apple Crisp

Overnight Honey-Wheat Rolls

Overnight Honey-Wheat Rolls

These easy yeast rolls don't require kneading, and the make-ahead dough saves you time on the day of your meal. I love the hint of honey, too. ~Lisa Varner, Greenville, South Carolina

    1 package (1/4 ounce) active dry yeast
1-1/4 cups warm water (110° to 115°), *divided*
    2 egg whites
    1/3 cup honey
    1/4 cup vegetable oil
    1 teaspoon salt
1-1/2 cups whole wheat flour
2-1/2 cups all-purpose flour
Melted butter, optional

1. In a small bowl, dissolve yeast in 1/4 cup warm water. In a large mixing bowl, beat egg whites until foamy. Add the yeast mixture, honey, oil, salt, whole wheat flour and remaining water. Beat on medium speed for 3 minutes or until smooth. Stir in enough all-purpose flour to form a soft dough (dough will be sticky). Cover and refrigerate overnight.

2. Punch dough down. Turn onto a well-floured surface; divide in half. Shape each portion into nine balls. To form knots, roll each ball into a 10-in. rope; tie into a knot. Tuck ends under. Place rolls 2 in. apart on greased baking sheets.

3. Cover and let rise until doubled, about 50 minutes. Bake at 375° for 10-12 minutes or until golden brown. Brush with melted butter if desired. **Yield:** 1-1/2 dozen.

Buttery Almond Green Beans

(Pictured on page 49)

Toasted almonds add crunch to this no-fuss treatment for fresh beans. They get extra flavor from convenient onion soup mix and Parmesan cheese. ~Edna Hoffman, Hebron, Indiana

    2 pounds fresh green beans, trimmed
    2 cups water
    1 envelope onion soup mix
  2/3 cup slivered almonds, toasted
    2 tablespoons grated Parmesan cheese
    1 teaspoon paprika
    6 tablespoons butter, melted

1. In a large saucepan, combine the beans, water and soup mix. Bring to a boil. Reduce heat; cover and simmer for 15-20 minutes or until beans are crisp-tender.

2. In a small bowl, combine the toasted almonds, Parmesan cheese and paprika. Drain the beans; drizzle with the melted butter and sprinkle with the almond mixture. Toss to coat. **Yield:** 8 servings.

Roasted Pepper and Olive Salad

When I was practicing roasting peppers, I tossed some on-hand ingredients together and came up with this recipe. It got rave reviews at our church potluck. ~Rick Salmon, Olathe, Kansas

    1 medium sweet red pepper
    1 medium sweet yellow pepper
    1 poblano pepper
    1 tablespoon olive oil
    1/2 teaspoon salt
    1/8 teaspoon pepper
1-1/2 cups torn fresh spinach
    1 large red onion, halved and sliced
    1 cup sliced fresh mushrooms
    1 large tomato, cut into wedges
    1 celery rib, thinly sliced
    1 can (3.8 ounces) sliced ripe olives, drained
  3/4 cup pimiento-stuffed olives, halved
DRESSING:
    1/4 cup red wine vinegar
    3 tablespoons olive oil
    2 tablespoons honey
  1/3 to 2/3 cup crumbled blue cheese
    1/3 cup minced fresh parsley

1. Halve peppers and remove seeds. Rub with oil; sprinkle with salt and pepper. Broil 4 in. from the heat until skins blister, about 4 minutes. Immediately place peppers in a bowl; cover and let stand for 15-20 minutes. Peel off and discard charred skin. Coarsely chop peppers.

2. In a large bowl, combine the peppers, spinach, onion, mushrooms, tomato, celery and olives. In a small bowl, combine the vinegar, oil and honey. Pour over vegetables and toss to coat. Sprinkle with blue cheese and parsley; gently toss to coat. Serve with a slotted spoon. **Yield:** 10 servings.

Parmesan Pastry Twists

These flaky, cheesy breadsticks go nicely with many different main courses. I serve the twists in a festive napkin-lined basket for the holidays. ~Hope Stinson, Louisville, Kentucky

1/2 cup grated Parmesan cheese
3/4 teaspoon coarsely ground pepper
1 garlic clove, minced
1 package (17.3 ounces) frozen puff pastry sheets, thawed
1 egg white, lightly beaten

1. In a small bowl, combine the Parmesan cheese, pepper and garlic. On a lightly floured surface, unfold one pastry sheet and brush with egg white. Sprinkle with a fourth of the Parmesan mixture; lightly press into pastry. Flip pastry sheet and repeat.

2. Cut sheet into 12 strips; cut each strip in half. Twist strips several times; place on greased baking sheets. Repeat with remaining pastry sheet. Bake at 350° for 14-16 minutes or until golden brown. **Yield:** 4 dozen.

Cranberry Raisin Relish

I'm not what you'd call an "expert" cook, but even I can make this! The fruit-filled relish is a colorful, tongue-tingling addition to Christmas dinner.   ~Barbara Ford, Fort Gratiot, Michigan

2 cups plus 2 tablespoons sugar
1/2 cup water
1/2 cup orange juice
2 cups fresh *or* frozen cranberries
1/2 cup chopped dried apricots
1/2 cup golden raisins
1-1/2 teaspoons grated orange peel

1. In a small saucepan, combine the sugar, water and orange juice; cook and stir over medium heat until the sugar is dissolved.

2. Stir in the cranberries, apricots, raisins and orange peel; bring to a boil. Reduce heat; cover and simmer until the berries pop, about 15 minutes. Serve relish warm or chilled. **Yield:** 2-1/2 cups.

Florets with Parmesan Sauce

For a simple but winning side dish, try this broccoli and cauliflower drizzled with a smooth sauce. I sprinkle extra Parmesan on top just before serving.   ~Jane Gregg, Bluffton, Indiana

4 cups fresh broccoli florets
4 cups fresh cauliflowerets
1 cup chicken broth
1/2 cup half-and-half cream
1/2 teaspoon Dijon mustard
3 tablespoons butter
3 tablespoons all-purpose flour
1/2 teaspoon onion powder
1/8 teaspoon white pepper
1/2 cup plus 2 tablespoons grated Parmesan cheese, *divided*

1. Place broccoli and cauliflower in a steamer basket; place in a saucepan over 1 in. of water. Bring to a boil; cover and steam for 5-8 minutes or until crisp-tender.

2. Meanwhile, in a small bowl, combine the broth, cream and mustard. In a small saucepan, melt butter. Stir in the flour, onion powder and pepper until smooth. Gradually stir in broth mixture. Bring to a boil; cook and stir for 2 minutes or until thickened. Remove from the heat. Stir in 1/2 cup Parmesan cheese.

3. Place vegetables in a serving bowl; drizzle with sauce and sprinkle with remaining Parmesan. **Yield:** 10 servings.

Mango-Berry Tossed Salad

Give your dinner a bit of tropical flair with this medley of mango, raspberries, avocado and greens. The colors are lovely on a holiday table.   ~Pam Peterson, Loveland, Colorado

3 tablespoons olive oil
2 tablespoons raspberry vinegar
2 tablespoons minced fresh parsley
1 tablespoon sugar
1 teaspoon poppy seeds
1 package (5 ounces) spring mix salad greens
3 cups fresh raspberries
1 medium mango, peeled and diced
1 medium ripe avocado, peeled and diced

For dressing, in a jar with a tight-fitting lid, combine the first five ingredients. Shake until sugar is dissolved. In a large bowl, combine the salad greens, raspberries, mango and avocado. Drizzle with dressing; toss gently to coat. Serve immediately. **Yield:** 8 servings.

Mango-Berry Tossed Salad

Truffle Torte

Delightful Desserts

★ *Whether your family is sweet on old-fashioned treats or new dessert temptations, they'll love this special collection for Christmastime.* ★

Truffle Torte

The biggest sweet tooths are satisfied with just a small slice of this rich, decadent torte. A white-chocolate pattern on top gives it an elegant finish. ~Mary Choate, Spring Hill, Florida

    3/4 cup butter, cubed
    8 squares (1 ounce *each*) semisweet chocolate,
        chopped
    6 eggs
    3/4 cup sugar
    1 teaspoon vanilla extract
    3/4 cup ground pecans
    1/4 cup all-purpose flour
GANACHE:
    1/2 cup heavy whipping cream
    4 squares (1 ounce *each*) semisweet chocolate,
        chopped
    2 tablespoons butter
GARNISH:
    2 squares (1 ounce *each*) white baking chocolate
    3/4 cup finely chopped pecans

1. Line the bottom of a greased 9-in. springform pan with waxed paper; grease the paper and set aside.

2. In a small saucepan, melt butter and chocolate over low heat. Cool. In a large mixing bowl, beat eggs until frothy; gradually add sugar, beating for 4-5 minutes or until mixture triples in volume. Gradually beat in chocolate mixture and vanilla. Combine pecans and flour; fold into batter. Pour into prepared pan.

3. Bake at 350° for 25-30 minutes or until cake springs back when lightly touched. Cool on a wire rack for 15 minutes. Run a knife around edge of pan; remove sides of pan. Invert cake onto wire rack; carefully remove pan bottom and waxed paper. Cool completely.

4. In a small heavy saucepan, heat the ganache ingredients over low heat, stirring until smooth. Remove from the heat. Cool, stirring occasionally, until ganache mixture reaches 85°-90°, about 15 minutes. Place the cooled cake on a serving plate. Pour the ganache over the cake and quickly spread ganache to edges of cake.

5. In a microwave-safe bowl, melt white chocolate; stir until smooth. Transfer to a heavy-duty resealable plastic bag; cut a small hole in a corner of bag. Pipe thin horizontal lines 1 in. apart over ganache. Use a sharp knife to draw right angles across the piped lines. Press pecans onto side of torte. Cover and refrigerate for 30 minutes or until set. Yield: 18 servings.

Lemon Pecan Pie

This unusual pie wins over everyone who tries it. The smooth filling nicely accents the nuts. ~Johnnie Williams, Mart, Texas

    1/2 cup butter, softened
    1 package (3 ounces) cream cheese, softened
    1/4 teaspoon butter flavoring
    1 cup all-purpose flour
FILLING:
    1-1/4 cups pecan halves
    1/2 cup packed brown sugar
    2 tablespoons all-purpose flour
    1 cup light corn syrup
    3 eggs
    1/3 cup butter, melted
    3 teaspoons lemon extract
    1 teaspoon butter flavoring
    1 teaspoon vanilla extract
    1/8 teaspoon salt

1. In a small mixing bowl, cream butter and cream cheese. Beat in flavoring. Gradually add flour until mixture forms a ball. Cover; refrigerate for 20 minutes or until easy to handle.

2. Roll out pastry to fit a 9-in. pie plate. Place pastry in plate; trim to 1/2 in. beyond edge of plate. Flute edges. Place pecans in crust; set aside.

3. In a small mixing bowl, combine brown sugar and flour. Add the remaining ingredients; beat until combined. Pour over pecans. Bake at 350° for 45-50 minutes or until a knife inserted near the center comes out clean. Cool completely on a wire rack. Refrigerate leftovers. Yield: 8 servings.

Lemon Pecan Pie

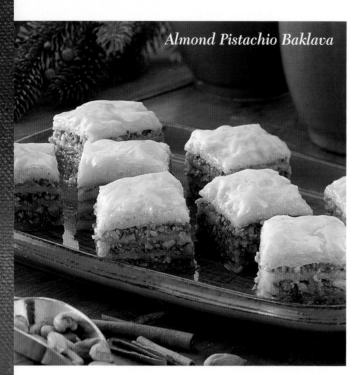
Almond Pistachio Baklava

Almond Pistachio Baklava

I discovered this traditional recipe at a Greek cultural event and often get requests for it. The original version called for walnuts, but I substituted almonds and pistachios with yummy results. ~Joan Lloyd, Barrie, Ontario

    3-3/4 cups sugar, *divided*
        2 cups water
        3/4 cup honey
        2 tablespoons lemon juice
        4 cups unsalted pistachios
        3 cups unsalted unblanched almonds
    1-1/2 teaspoons ground cinnamon
        1/2 teaspoon ground nutmeg
    1-3/4 cups butter, melted
        3 packages (16 ounces *each*, 14-inch x 9-inch sheet size) frozen phyllo dough, thawed

1. In a small saucepan, bring 2-3/4 cups sugar, water, honey and lemon juice to a boil. Reduce heat; simmer for 5 minutes. Cool.

2. In a food processor, combine pistachios and almonds; cover and process until finely chopped. Transfer to a bowl. Stir in the cinnamon, nutmeg and remaining sugar; set aside. Brush a 15-in. x 10-in. x 1-in. baking pan with some of the butter. Unroll one package of phyllo dough; cut stack into a 10-1/2-in. x 9-in. rectangle. Repeat with remaining phyllo. Discard scraps.

3. Line bottom of prepared pan with two sheets of phyllo dough (sheets will overlap slightly). Brush with butter. Repeat layers 14 times. (Keep dough covered with plastic wrap and a damp towel until ready to use to prevent it from drying out.) Sprinkle with a third of the nut mixture.

4. Top with 15 layers of buttered phyllo dough and a third of the nut mixture; repeat layers. Top with remaining phyllo dough, buttering each layer.

5. Using a sharp knife, cut into 1-1/2-in. diamond shapes. Bake at 350° for 35-40 minutes or until golden brown. Place pan on a wire rack. Slowly pour cooled sugar syrup over baklava. Cover and let stand overnight. **Yield:** about 4 dozen.

Walnut Spice Fruitcake

I'm really glad I tried this recipe, and you will be, too! I think it tastes like a cross between classic Christmas fruitcake and homemade spice cake. ~Vada Price, Madison, West Virginia

        1 cup raisins
        1 cup chopped walnuts
        1 cup red candied cherries, halved
        1 cup shortening
        1 cup sugar
        2 eggs
    3-1/2 cups all-purpose flour
        2 teaspoons baking soda
        2 teaspoons ground cinnamon
        1 teaspoon salt
        1/2 to 3/4 teaspoon ground cloves
        1/2 to 3/4 teaspoon ground nutmeg
        2 cups sweetened applesauce
    TOPPING:
        24 red *and/or* green candied cherries
        1/4 cup walnut halves

1. In a large bowl, combine the raisins, walnuts and cherries; set aside. In a large mixing bowl, cream shortening and sugar until light and fluffy. Add eggs, one at a time, beating well after each addition.

2. Combine the flour, baking soda, cinnamon, salt, cloves and nutmeg; add to creamed mixture alternately with applesauce. Mix well. Stir in the raisin mixture. Transfer to a greased and floured 10-in. tube pan; top with whole cherries and walnut halves.

3. Bake at 325° for 1-1/2 hours or until a toothpick inserted near the center comes out clean. Cool for 10 minutes before removing from pan to a wire rack to cool completely. Wrap tightly and store in a cool dry place. **Yield:** 12-16 servings.

Steamed Cranberry-Molasses Pudding

This old-fashioned dessert has been a family tradition during the holidays for years. My children say it's just not Christmas without it! ~Millicent Tilly, Watertown, South Dakota

    1-1/3 cups all-purpose flour
        2 teaspoons baking soda
        1 teaspoon baking powder
        1/2 cup molasses
        1/3 cup hot water
        2 cups chopped fresh *or* frozen cranberries
    BUTTER SAUCE:
        1/2 cup butter, cubed
        1 cup sugar
        1 cup heavy whipping cream

1. In a large bowl, combine the flour, baking soda and baking powder. Combine molasses and water; stir into dry ingredients. Fold in cranberries. Pour into a well-greased 4-cup pudding mold; cover.

2. Place mold on a rack in a deep kettle; add 1 in. of hot water to pan. Bring to a gentle boil; cover and steam for 1 hour or until a toothpick inserted near the center comes out clean, adding water to pan as needed. Let stand for 5 minutes before removing from mold.

3. In a small saucepan, melt butter; stir in sugar and heavy whipping cream. Cook and stir over medium heat for 3-5 minutes or until heated through. Unmold pudding onto a serving plate; cut into wedges. Serve warm with butter sauce. Yield: 8-10 servings.

Cranberry Cheesecake Dessert

I'm always asked to bring this memorable layered dessert to Christmas parties, and I'm happy to oblige. People rave about the combination of rich cheesecake, tangy cranberries and chewy coconut. ~Helen Helm, Gig Harbor, Washington

1-1/4 cups all-purpose flour
  1/2 cup packed brown sugar
  1/2 cup cold butter
  1/2 cup finely chopped walnuts
  1/4 cup flaked coconut
FILLING:
  2 packages (8 ounces *each*) cream cheese, softened
  2/3 cup sugar
  2 eggs, lightly beaten
  2 teaspoons vanilla extract
TOPPING:
  1 can (16 ounces) whole-berry cranberry sauce
  1/2 cup coarsely chopped walnuts
  1/2 cup flaked coconut

1. For the crust, in a large bowl, combine the flour and brown sugar; cut in the butter until crumbly. Stir in the walnuts and coconut. Press the mixture into a greased 13-in. x 9-in. x 2-in. baking dish. Bake at 350° for 12-15 minutes or until lightly browned.

2. Meanwhile, in a large mixing bowl, beat cream cheese and sugar until smooth. Add eggs and vanilla; beat on low speed just until combined. Spread evenly over crust. Bake for 15 minutes.

3. Spoon cranberry sauce over filling; sprinkle with walnuts and coconut. Bake 15-20 minutes longer or until top is lightly browned. Cool completely on a wire rack. Refrigerate until chilled. Yield: 15 servings.

Mocha Cream Torte

My guests never guess that this impressive chocolate dessert relies on a packaged cake mix. Mocha flavor and cream cheese frosting make it special. ~Mary Lohse, Chatfield, Minnesota

1-1/2 cups graham cracker crumbs
  3/4 cup packed brown sugar
  1/2 cup butter, melted
  1/2 cup chopped walnuts
  1 tablespoon mocha-flavored coffee drink mix
  1 package (18-1/4 ounces) dark chocolate cake mix
FROSTING:
  1 package (8 ounces) cream cheese, softened
  2 tablespoons butter, softened
  2 tablespoons sour cream
  3 tablespoons mocha-flavored coffee drink mix
  4 cups confectioners' sugar

1. Grease and flour three 9-in. round baking pans. Line bottoms with waxed paper; grease and flour the paper. In a small bowl, combine the cracker crumbs, brown sugar, butter, walnuts and drink mix; press into prepared pans.

2. Prepare cake batter according to package directions; pour over prepared crusts. Bake according to package directions. Cool for 10 minutes; remove from pans to wire racks to cool completely. Remove waxed paper.

3. For frosting, in a large mixing bowl, beat the cream cheese, butter, sour cream and drink mix until fluffy. Add confectioners' sugar; beat until smooth. Place one cake layer, crunchy side up, on a serving plate. Spread with 3/4 cup frosting. Repeat with remaining layers and frosting. Store in the refrigerator. Yield: 12-16 servings.

Editor's Note: This recipe was tested with Pillsbury dark chocolate cake mix.

Mocha Cream Torte

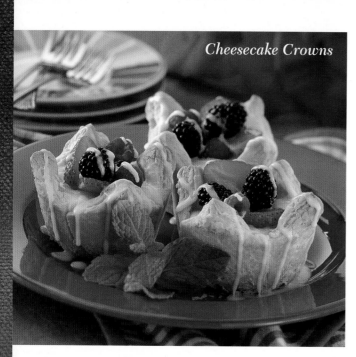

Cheesecake Crowns

crowns with fresh berries if desired; drizzle with glaze. Refrigerate leftovers. **Yield: 1 dozen.**

Strawberry Malted Mousse Cups

Eyes light up whenever I bring these pretty treats to the table. The mousse cups are nice not only for Christmas, but also for bridal and baby showers. ~Anna Ginsberg, Austin, Texas

    1 package (3 ounces) strawberry gelatin
    1 tablespoon cornstarch
    1 cup water
1/4 cup malted milk powder
    1 cup refrigerated French vanilla nondairy creamer
    1 carton (8 ounces) frozen whipped topping, thawed, *divided*
Fresh strawberries and mint, optional

1. In a small saucepan, combine the gelatin, cornstarch and water until smooth. Bring to a boil; cook and stir for 3-5 minutes or until mixture becomes clear. Remove from the heat; cool for 5 minutes.

2. In a small bowl, combine malted milk powder and creamer; whisk into gelatin mixture. Stir in 2 cups whipped topping. Spoon into six dessert dishes; chill until set.

3. Just before serving, dollop with remaining whipped topping. Garnish with berries and mint if desired. **Yield: 6 servings.**

Cheesecake Crowns

These elegant dessert pastries are so easy to make, but no one will believe it! I've served the fruit-filled crowns at brunch as well as after dinner. ~Brenda Westra, Kalamazoo, Michigan

    2 packages (17.3 ounces *each*) frozen puff pastry, thawed
1/2 cup all-purpose flour
1/2 cup finely chopped pecans
1/4 cup packed brown sugar
1/2 teaspoon ground cinnamon
1/4 cup cold butter
    3 packages (8 ounces *each*) cream cheese, softened
    1 cup sugar
    3 eggs, lightly beaten
    6 teaspoons vanilla extract
1/4 cup confectioners' sugar
1-1/2 to 2 teaspoons water
Fresh raspberries, blackberries and sliced fresh strawberries, optional

1. Thaw three puff pastry sheets (save remaining sheet for another use). Unfold pastry; cut each into four squares. Gently press squares into greased jumbo muffin cups, pulling corners up and out of cups; press corners down onto muffin pan.

2. In a small bowl, combine the flour, pecans, brown sugar and cinnamon. Cut in butter until crumbly. Sprinkle 1 heaping tablespoonful into each muffin cup.

3. In a large mixing bowl, beat cream cheese and sugar until smooth. Beat in eggs on low speed just until combined. Stir in vanilla. Spoon into pastry cups.

4. Bake at 400° for 20-25 minutes or until filling is almost set and pastry is golden brown. Cool completely on wire racks. Refrigerate, uncovered, for 1 hour or until set.

5. For glaze, in a small bowl, combine confectioners' sugar and enough water to achieve a drizzling consistency. Garnish

Raspberry-Swirl Cheesecake Pie

This attractive pie is a favorite of mine for family gatherings. But I have to bake more than one because some of my relatives worry that they won't get a piece! ~Gusty Crum, Dover, Ohio

    1 package (8 ounces) cream cheese, softened
    1 tablespoon all-purpose flour
    1 can (14 ounces) sweetened condensed milk
    3 tablespoons plus 1 teaspoon lemon juice, *divided*
    1 egg, lightly beaten
    1 graham cracker crust (9 inches)
1/2 cup seedless raspberry preserves
Fresh raspberries and mint, optional

1. In a small mixing bowl, beat cream cheese and flour until smooth. Beat in milk and 3 tablespoons lemon juice. Add egg; beat on low speed just until combined. Pour half of the filling into crust.

2. In a small bowl, combine preserves and remaining lemon juice. Drop two-thirds of the mixture by teaspoonfuls over filling; cut through with a knife to swirl. Top with remaining filling and preserves; cut through with a knife to swirl.

3. Bake at 300° for 50-60 minutes or until center is almost set. Cool on a wire rack for 1 hour. Refrigerate until chilled. **Yield: 6-8 servings.**

Raspberry-Swirl Cheesecake Pie
Strawberry Malted Mousse Cups

Jalapeno Cranberry Chutney
Raspberry-Pecan Mini Loaves (p. 60)
Deluxe Spiced Tea Mix (p. 60)

Gifts of Good Cheer

★ *Wrap up your holiday gift-giving in the kitchen with these homemade specialties, from chocolate-coated candies to spicy cheese snacks.* ★

Jalapeno Cranberry Chutney

This crimson-colored chutney from our Test Kitchen staff makes a tongue-tingling Christmas gift. Serve it with crackers as an appetizer or with turkey or chicken as a condiment.

2-1/4 cups packed brown sugar
1-1/2 cups water
  1/2 cup white vinegar
  3/4 teaspoon curry powder
  1/2 teaspoon ground ginger
  1/2 teaspoon ground cinnamon
  1/4 teaspoon ground cloves
  1/4 teaspoon ground allspice
   2 medium navel oranges
   2 medium lemons
   1 medium tart apple, peeled and chopped
   1 jalapeno pepper, seeded and minced
   6 cups fresh *or* frozen cranberries, *divided*
  1/2 cup golden raisins
  1/2 cup dried apricots, chopped
  1/2 cup chopped walnuts

1. In a large saucepan, combine the first eight ingredients. Bring to a boil, stirring occasionally. Grate the peel from the oranges and lemons; add to sugar mixture. Peel off and discard pith from oranges and lemons; chop pulp and add to sugar mixture. Stir in apple and jalapeno. Bring to a boil. Reduce heat; simmer, uncovered, for 10 minutes.

2. Add 3 cups cranberries, raisins and apricots. Bring to a boil. Reduce heat; simmer, uncovered, for 30 minutes, stirring occasionally. Add remaining cranberries. Bring to a boil. Reduce heat; simmer, uncovered, 15 minutes longer.

3. Stir in walnuts. Serve warm or chilled. Pour into refrigerator or freezer containers. Refrigerate for up to 3 weeks or freeze for up to 12 months. **Yield:** 4 pints.

Editor's Note: When cutting or seeding hot peppers, use rubber or plastic gloves to protect your hands. Avoid touching your face.

Cranberry Swirl Biscotti

A friend of mine, who is known for her excellent cookies, shared this recipe with me. The mix of cranberries and cherry preserves is so refreshing. ~Lisa Kilcup, Gig Harbor, Washington

  2/3 cup dried cranberries
  1/2 cup cherry preserves
  1/2 teaspoon ground cinnamon
  1/2 cup butter, softened
  2/3 cup sugar
   2 eggs
   1 teaspoon vanilla extract
2-1/4 cups all-purpose flour
  3/4 teaspoon baking powder
  1/4 teaspoon salt
GLAZE:
  3/4 cup confectioners' sugar
   1 tablespoon milk
   2 teaspoons butter, melted
   1 teaspoon almond extract

1. In a food processor, combine the cranberries, preserves and cinnamon. Cover and process until smooth; set aside.

2. In a large mixing bowl, cream butter and sugar. Beat in eggs and vanilla. Combine the flour, baking powder and salt; gradually add to creamed mixture and mix well.

3. Divide dough in half. On a lightly floured surface, roll each half into a 12-in. x 8-in. rectangle. Spread each with berry filling; roll up jelly-roll style, starting with a short side. Place seam side down 4 in. apart on a lightly greased baking sheet. Bake at 325° for 25-30 minutes or until lightly browned.

4. Using two large metal spatulas, carefully transfer logs to a cutting board; cool for 5 minutes. With a serrated knife, cut into 1/2-in. slices. Place 2 in. apart on lightly greased baking sheets. Bake 15 minutes longer or until centers are firm and dry. Remove to wire racks.

5. In a small bowl, combine glaze ingredients; drizzle over warm biscotti. Cool completely. Store in an airtight container. **Yield:** about 2-1/2 dozen.

Cranberry Swirl Biscotti

Parmesan Pretzel Rods

1/2 teaspoon salt
1/4 teaspoon baking soda
2 eggs
1/2 cup vanilla yogurt
1/3 cup orange juice
1/4 cup unsweetened applesauce
1/4 cup vegetable oil
1/2 teaspoon orange extract
1 cup chopped pecans, toasted
1 cup fresh *or* frozen raspberries

GLAZE:
1 cup confectioners' sugar
4 to 5 teaspoons orange juice

1. In a large bowl, combine the flour, sugar, baking powder, salt and baking soda. In a small bowl, whisk the eggs, yogurt, orange juice, applesauce, oil and extract. Stir into dry ingredients just until moistened. Fold in pecans and raspberries.

2. Transfer to six greased 4-1/2-in. x 2-1/2-in. x 1-1/2-in. loaf pans. Bake at 350° for 25-28 minutes or until a toothpick inserted near the center comes out clean. Cool for 10 minutes before removing from pans to wire racks.

3. For glaze, combine confectioners' sugar and enough orange juice to achieve desired consistency. Drizzle over loaves. Yield: 6 mini loaves.

Editor's Note: If using frozen raspberries, do not thaw before adding to batter.

Parmesan Pretzel Rods

For the snack fans on your gift list, these cheesy pretzels are terrific. The coated rods get great flavor from garlic powder, oregano and cayenne. ~Cindy Winter-Hartley, Cary, North Carolina

1 cup grated Parmesan cheese
1 teaspoon garlic powder
1 teaspoon dried oregano
1/2 teaspoon cayenne pepper
6 tablespoons butter
1/4 cup olive oil
1 package (10 ounces) pretzel rods

1. In a small bowl, combine the Parmesan cheese, garlic powder, oregano and cayenne; set aside. In a small saucepan, heat butter and oil until butter is melted. Coat two-thirds of each pretzel rod with butter mixture, then roll in cheese mixture. Reheat butter mixture if needed.

2. Place in an ungreased 15-in. x 10-in. x 1-in. baking pan. Bake at 275° for 20-25 minutes or until golden brown, turning once. Cool. Store in an airtight container. Yield: about 2-1/2 dozen.

Raspberry-Pecan Mini Loaves

(Pictured on page 58)

Dotted with raspberries and pecans, these moist loaves make lovely Christmas treats. The recipe yields six, so you'll have plenty to share. ~Kathleen Showalter, Shoreline, Washington

2 cups all-purpose flour
1/2 cup sugar
2 teaspoons baking powder

Deluxe Spiced Tea Mix

(Pictured on page 58)

During the holiday season, a jar of this spicy-sweet tea mix always goes over well. A steaming mug is a wonderful way to warm up on chilly mornings. ~Deanie Milligan, Carrollton, Texas

2 jars (21.1 ounces *each*) orange breakfast drink mix
1 cup sugar
1 envelope (5 ounces) sweetened lemonade drink mix
1 jar (3 ounces) unsweetened instant tea
2-1/4 cups red-hot candies
2 teaspoons *each* ground allspice, cinnamon, cloves and nutmeg

1. In an airtight container, combine all ingredients. Store in a cool dry place up to 6 months. Yield: 10 cups (about 120 servings).

2. To prepare tea: Dissolve 4 teaspoons mix in 1 cup boiling water; stir well. Yield: 1 serving.

No-Bake Mallow Fruitcake

When my granddaughter made plans to visit friends in Norway at Christmastime, they asked her for an "American Christmas cake." We realized they meant fruitcake and chose this yummy version. They loved it! ~Marge Gansen, Lecanto, Florida

1 package (16 ounces) graham crackers
1 package (15 ounces) raisins

1 pound red *or* green candied cherries
1/2 pound chopped candied pineapple
2 cups whole Brazil nuts
2 cups walnut halves
3/4 cup milk
1 package (16 ounces) large marshmallows

1. Line two 8-in. x 4-in. x 2-in. pans with foil and grease the foil; set aside. Crush graham crackers until fine crumbs form; place in a large bowl. Add the raisins, cherries, pineapple and nuts; set aside.

2. In a large saucepan, heat milk and marshmallows over low heat until marshmallows are melted; stir until blended. Pour over fruit mixture and stir until well blended. Divide between prepared pans, packing down firmly. Cover with foil; refrigerate for at least 1 week before serving. **Yield:** 2 loaves.

Gimme More Snack Mix

My beautician gave me the recipe for this sweet-salty snack, and it was an immediate hit with my family. The mix didn't have a name, so we came up with one that seemed perfect—"gimme more!" ~Mary Ellen Hutton, Curwensville, Pennsylvania

6 cups Rice Chex
6 cups Cheerios
1 can (12 ounces) salted peanuts
1 package (12 ounces) miniature pretzels
1 pound white candy coating, coarsely chopped
2 packages (10 ounces *each*) peanut butter chips
3 tablespoons vegetable oil

1. In a large bowl, combine the cereals, peanuts and pretzels; set aside. In a large microwave-safe bowl, melt the candy coating, peanut butter chips and oil; stir until smooth. Pour over cereal mixture and stir to coat.

2. Spread onto waxed paper-lined baking sheets; let stand until set. Break into pieces. Store in an airtight container. **Yield:** about 4-1/2 pounds.

Date-Pecan Coconut Candy

This fuss-free recipe has been in our family for years. A batch of these chocolate-covered balls always brings back wonderful holiday memories. ~Eileen Balmer, South Bend, Indiana

1 pound pitted dates, chopped
2 cups chopped pecans
1 package (16 ounces) miniature marshmallows
6 cups flaked coconut
3 packages (12 ounces *each*) semisweet chocolate chips
2 tablespoons shortening

1. In a large bowl, combine the dates, pecans, marshmallows and coconut. In a blender or food processor, process date mixture in batches. Shape into 1-in. balls.

2. In a microwave-safe bowl, melt chocolate chips and shortening; stir until smooth. Dip balls into chocolate; allow excess

to drip off. Place on waxed paper to harden. Store in an airtight container. **Yield:** about 6 dozen.

Double-Nut English Toffee

You'll have plenty of goodies on hand when you make this nut-packed candy. Unlike some versions, this toffee isn't too hard and is easy to eat. ~Lucie Fitzgerald, Spring Hill, Florida

1-1/2 teaspoons plus 2 cups butter, softened, *divided*
2 cups sugar
1 cup chopped almonds, toasted
1 package (12 ounces) semisweet chocolate chips, *divided*
2 cups ground walnuts *or* pecans, *divided*

1. Butter a 15-in. x 10-in. x 1-in. pan with 1-1/2 teaspoons butter; set aside. In a heavy saucepan, combine sugar and remaining butter. Cook and stir over medium heat until a candy thermometer reads 290° (soft-crack stage). Remove from the heat; stir in almonds. Immediately pour into prepared pan.

2. Sprinkle with 1 cup chocolate chips; let stand until chips become glossy. Spread evenly over top. Sprinkle with 1 cup walnuts. Cover and refrigerate until set, about 1 hour.

3. In a microwave-safe bowl, melt remaining chips; stir until smooth. Spread over toffee. Sprinkle with remaining walnuts. Cover and refrigerate until set, about 30 minutes. Break toffee into 2-in. pieces. Store in an airtight container. **Yield:** 3-1/2 pounds.

Editor's Note: We recommend that you test your candy thermometer before each use by bringing water to a boil; the thermometer should read 212°. Adjust your recipe temperature up or down based on your test.

Double-Nut English Toffee

Slice 'n' Bake Fruitcake Cookies (p. 64)
Chocolate Walnut Crescents (p. 64)
Nativity Molasses Cookies

Merry Cookies

★ *Frosted cutouts, sprinkled spritz, chocolaty crescents...all kinds of delectable delights for Christmastime are featured for you here.* ★

Nativity Molasses Cookies

You'll have seasonal spirit well in hand when you cut out these chewy cookies in lamb, camel, star, angel and other Nativity-themed shapes. A simple, homemade white icing is the perfect finishing touch. ~Nancy Amann, Fountain City, Wisconsin

　1/2 cup shortening
　1/2 cup sugar
　　1 egg yolk
　1/2 cup water
　1/2 cup molasses
3-1/4 cups all-purpose flour
　　1 teaspoon baking soda
　1/2 teaspoon salt
　1/2 teaspoon ground ginger
　1/2 teaspoon ground cinnamon
　1/2 teaspoon ground cloves
ICING:
　3/4 cup sugar
　　1 egg white
　1/3 cup water
　1/8 teaspoon cream of tartar

1. In a large mixing bowl, cream shortening and sugar. Beat in the egg yolk, water and molasses. Combine the flour, baking soda, salt, ginger, cinnamon and cloves; gradually add to creamed mixture and mix well. Cover and refrigerate for 2 hours or until easy to handle.

2. On a lightly floured surface, roll out dough to 1/8-in. thickness. Cut with floured 2-1/2-in. Nativity-themed cookie cutters. Place 1 in. apart on ungreased baking sheets. Bake at 350° for 10-12 minutes or until edges are firm. Remove to wire racks to cool completely.

3. In a heavy saucepan over low heat, combine the icing ingredients. With a portable mixer, beat on low speed for 1 minute. Continue beating over low heat until frosting reaches 160°, about 8-10 minutes. Pour into a small mixing bowl. Beat on high speed until icing forms stiff peaks, about 7 minutes. Spread over cookies; let dry completely. Yield: 5 dozen.

Editor's Note: A stand mixer is recommended for beating the frosting after it reaches 160°.

Lemon Spritz

My mother made these yummy tinted cookies at Christmastime, and she always baked a big batch. My sister, brothers and I had lots of fun decorating them with colored sprinkles...and sampling them, too! ~Brenda Viozzi, Palmyra, Pennsylvania

　　1 cup shortening
　　1 package (3 ounces) cream cheese, softened
　　1 cup sugar
　　1 egg yolk
　　1 teaspoon vanilla extract
　　1 teaspoon grated lemon peel
2-1/2 cups all-purpose flour
　1/2 teaspoon salt
　1/4 teaspoon ground cinnamon
Food coloring, optional
Nonpareils and colored sugar, optional

1. In a large mixing bowl, cream the shortening, cream cheese and sugar. Beat in egg yolk, vanilla and lemon peel. Combine the flour, salt and cinnamon; gradually add to creamed mixture. Beat in food coloring if desired. Cover and refrigerate for 30 minutes or until easy to handle.

2. Using a cookie press fitted with the disk of your choice, press dough 2 in. apart onto ungreased baking sheets. Sprinkle with nonpareils and colored sugar if desired. Bake at 350° for 12-15 minutes or until set (do not brown). Remove to wire racks. Yield: about 9 dozen.

Lemon Spritz

Cherry Pecan Dreams

Cherry Pecan Dreams

Packed with fruit, nuts and vanilla chips, these goodies are sure to please. If you prefer, replace the cherries with cranberries or apricots. ~Mary Ann Mariotti, Plainfield, Illinois

1 cup butter, softened
1/2 cup sugar
1/2 cup packed brown sugar
1 egg
1 tablespoon grated orange peel
2-1/4 cups all-purpose flour
1 teaspoon baking soda
1/2 teaspoon salt
2 cups vanilla *or* white chips
1 cup dried cherries, coarsely chopped
1 cup chopped pecans

1. In a large mixing bowl, cream butter and sugars. Beat in egg and orange peel. Combine the flour, baking soda and salt; gradually add to creamed mixture and mix well. Fold in the chips, cherries and pecans.

2. Drop by rounded tablespoonfuls 2 in. apart onto greased baking sheets. Bake at 350° for 10-12 minutes or until edges are golden brown. Cool for 2 minutes before removing to wire racks. **Yield:** about 3 dozen.

Chocolate Walnut Crescents

(Pictured on page 62)

I use a round cookie cutter to form the crescent shapes for these nutty favorites. They're so pretty sprinkled with sugar and drizzled with chocolate. ~TerryAnn Moore, Oaklyn, New Jersey

1 cup butter, softened
1/2 cup sugar
1 teaspoon vanilla extract
2 cups all-purpose flour
2 cups ground walnuts
3 tablespoons baking cocoa

2 to 3 tablespoons confectioners' sugar
1 package (12 ounces) semisweet chocolate chips
2 teaspoons shortening

1. In a large mixing bowl, cream butter and sugar. Beat in vanilla. Combine the flour, walnuts and cocoa; gradually add to creamed mixture and mix well. Cover and refrigerate for 1 hour or until easy to handle.

2. On a lightly floured surface, roll out dough to 1/4-in. thickness. Using a floured, plain or finely scalloped 2-in. round cookie cutter, cut a semicircle off one corner of the dough, forming the inside of a crescent shape. Reposition cutter 1-1/4 in. from inside of crescent; cut cookie, forming a crescent 1-1/4 in. wide at its widest point. Repeat. Chill and reroll scraps if desired.

3. Place 1 in. apart on ungreased baking sheets. Bake at 350° for 9-11 minutes or until set. Cool for 1 minute before removing to wire racks to cool completely.

4. Sprinkle cookies with confectioners' sugar. In a microwave-safe bowl, melt chocolate chips and shortening; stir until smooth. Drizzle over cookies; let stand until set. Store in an airtight container. **Yield:** 10-1/2 dozen.

Slice 'n' Bake Fruitcake Cookies

(Pictured on page 62)

A cross between classic fruitcake and buttery cookies, these treats are perfect for Christmas. Each one is chock-full of raisins and candied cherries. ~Marlene Robinson, Sexsmith, Alberta

1 cup butter, softened
1 cup confectioners' sugar
1/2 cup sugar
1 egg
2 teaspoons vanilla extract
2-1/4 cups all-purpose flour
1/2 teaspoon baking soda
1/2 cup raisins
1/2 cup *each* red and green candied cherries, chopped

1. In a large mixing bowl, cream butter and sugars until light and fluffy. Beat in egg and vanilla. Combine flour and baking soda; gradually add to creamed mixture and mix well. Fold in raisins and cherries.

2. Shape dough into two 2-in.-thick logs; wrap each in plastic wrap. Refrigerate for 2 hours or until firm.

3. Cut logs into 1/4-in. slices. Place 2 in. apart on ungreased baking sheets. Bake at 350° for 12-15 minutes or until lightly browned. Remove to wire racks to cool. **Yield:** 5 dozen.

No-Bake Cookie Balls

These quick bites are great when you're short on time or don't want to turn on the oven. I make them a day or two ahead to let the flavors blend. ~Carmeletta Dailey, Winfield, Texas

1 cup (6 ounces) semisweet chocolate chips
3 cups confectioners' sugar
1-3/4 cups crushed vanilla wafers (about 50 wafers)
1 cup chopped walnuts, toasted
1/3 cup orange juice
3 tablespoons light corn syrup
Additional confectioners' sugar

In a large microwave-safe bowl, melt chocolate chips; stir until smooth. Stir in the confectioners' sugar, vanilla wafers, walnuts, orange juice and corn syrup. Roll into 1-in. balls; roll in additional confectioners' sugar. Store in an airtight container. Yield: 5 dozen.

Lebkuchen

It's tradition for my family to get together on Thanksgiving weekend and bake these spice-filled treats. The recipe came from my great-grandmother. ~Esther Kempker, Jefferson City, Missouri

1/2 cup butter, softened
1/2 cup sugar
1/3 cup packed brown sugar
1 cup molasses
1/4 cup buttermilk
2 eggs
4-1/2 cups all-purpose flour
1-1/2 teaspoons baking powder
1 teaspoon baking soda
1 teaspoon ground cinnamon
1/2 teaspoon salt
1/2 teaspoon *each* ground cloves, allspice and
    cardamom
1/2 cup ground walnuts
1/2 cup raisins
1/2 cup pitted dates
1/2 cup candied lemon peel
1/3 cup flaked coconut
1/4 cup candied orange peel
3 tablespoons candied pineapple
1/2 teaspoon anise extract
GLAZE:
1 cup sugar
2 tablespoons hot water
1/4 teaspoon vanilla extract

1. Line a 15-in. x 10-in. x 1-in. baking pan with foil; grease the foil and set aside. In a large mixing bowl, cream butter and sugars. Beat in molasses and buttermilk. Add eggs, one at a time, beating well after each. Combine the flour, baking powder, baking soda, cinnamon, salt, cloves, allspice and cardamom; gradually add to creamed mixture. Stir in walnuts.

2. In a food processor, grind the raisins, dates, lemon peel, coconut, orange peel and candied pineapple in batches. Stir into the batter. Add anise extract. Press the dough into the prepared pan.

3. Bake at 350° for 25-28 minutes or until lightly browned. Combine the glaze ingredients; spread over warm bars. Immediately cut into squares. Cool in the pan on a wire rack. Yield: 3 dozen.

Cream Cheese Brownies

Brownies are a common dessert in our household—they're just about the only form of chocolate my husband will eat! I love this version that makes a big batch and has a rich cream-cheese layer in the center. ~Barbara Nitcznski, Denver, Colorado

1/2 cup butter, cubed
4 squares (1 ounce *each*) unsweetened chocolate
4 eggs
2 cups sugar
2 teaspoons vanilla extract
1-1/2 cups all-purpose flour
1 cup chopped nuts, optional
FILLING:
2 packages (8 ounces *each*) cream cheese, softened
1/2 cup sugar
1 egg
2 teaspoons vanilla extract

1. In a small saucepan, melt butter and chocolate over low heat; stir until smooth. Remove from the heat; set aside.

2. In a large mixing bowl, beat eggs. Gradually add sugar, beating until thick and light lemon-colored. Beat in vanilla. Add flour and mix well. Stir in melted chocolate and nuts if desired (batter will be thick). Spread half of the batter evenly into a greased 13-in. x 9-in. x 2-in. baking pan; set aside.

3. For filling, in a small mixing bowl, beat cream cheese and sugar until light and fluffy. Add egg and vanilla; mix well. Gently spread over batter. Spoon remaining batter over filling; spread to cover.

4. Bake at 350° for 45-50 minutes or until a toothpick inserted near the center comes out clean. Cool on a wire rack. Cut into bars. Store in the refrigerator. Yield: 4 dozen.

Cream Cheese Brownies

Apricot Coconut Treasures

Apricot Coconut Treasures

These elegant filled cookies are some of my favorites for Christ-mastime. Try them for a bridal shower, spring brunch or ladies' luncheon, too. ~Helen Keber, Oshkosh, Wisconsin

    1 cup butter, softened
    1 cup (8 ounces) sour cream
    2 cups all-purpose flour
  1/2 teaspoon salt
  1/2 cup flaked coconut
  1/2 cup apricot preserves
  1/4 cup chopped walnuts

1. In a large mixing bowl, cream butter and sour cream. Combine flour and salt; gradually add to creamed mixture. Divide dough into fourths; wrap in plastic wrap. Refrigerate for 4 hours or until easy to handle.

2. In a small bowl, combine the coconut, preserves and walnuts; set aside. On a lightly floured surface, roll out each portion of dough to 1/8-in. thickness. Cut into 2-1/2-in. squares; spread each with a rounded teaspoonful of coconut mixture. Carefully fold one corner over filling. Moisten opposite corner with water and fold over first corner; seal.

3. Place 1-1/2 in. apart on ungreased baking sheets. Bake at 350° for 18-20 minutes or until lightly browned. Remove to wire racks to cool. **Yield:** 2-1/2 dozen.

Snowcapped Chocolate Cookies

If you like chocolate, you'll love these kiss-shaped, crinkled cookies. They get their "snowcapped" look from a coating of confectioners' sugar. ~Rayla Molzon, DeWitt, Michigan

  1/2 cup butter, softened
    2 cups sugar
    4 eggs
    4 squares (1 ounce *each*) unsweetened chocolate, melted
    2 teaspoons vanilla extract
2-1/2 cups all-purpose flour
    2 teaspoons baking powder
  3/4 teaspoon salt
    1 cup confectioners' sugar

1. In a large mixing bowl, cream butter and sugar until light and fluffy. Add eggs, one at a time, beating well after each addition. Beat in chocolate and vanilla. Combine flour, baking powder and salt; gradually add to creamed mixture and mix well. Cover and refrigerate for 3 hours or until easy to handle.

2. Place confectioners' sugar in a shallow bowl; drop dough by rounded teaspoonfuls into sugar. Coat with sugar and form into teardrop shapes. Place 2 in. apart on greased baking sheets. Bake at 350° for 8-10 minutes or until set. Remove to wire racks. **Yield:** about 7 dozen.

Marbled Greeting Cookies

These festive goodies are like little Christmas cards with holiday wishes for your guests. Using a fluted pastry wheel gives the edges a pretty, ruffled finish. ~Darlene Brenden, Salem, Oregon

  1/2 cup butter, softened
  1/3 cup shortening
    1 cup sugar
    1 egg
  1/3 cup sour cream
    1 teaspoon vanilla extract
2-1/2 cups all-purpose flour
  3/4 teaspoon baking powder
  1/4 teaspoon baking soda
  1/8 teaspoon salt
Red and green food coloring
    1 tube white decorating gel

1. In a large mixing bowl, cream the butter, shortening and sugar. Beat in egg, sour cream and vanilla. Combine the flour, baking powder, baking soda and salt; gradually add to creamed mixture and mix well.

2. Divide dough into thirds. Tint one portion red and one portion green; leave one portion plain. Wrap in plastic wrap; chill for 30 minutes or until easy to handle.

3. Drop dough by tablespoonfuls, randomly alternating colors, onto a lightly floured surface. Press together, forming a 13-in. x 4-1/2-in. rectangle. Roll out dough to 1/4-in. thickness, forming a 15-in. x 8-in. rectangle. Using a fluted pastry wheel, cut dough in half lengthwise. Cut each half into 12 strips measuring 4 in. x 1-1/4 in.

4. Place 2 in. apart on ungreased baking sheets. Bake at 375° for 10-12 minutes or until set. Cool for 2 minutes before removing to wire racks to cool completely. Use decorating gel to write greetings on cookies. **Yield:** 2 dozen.

hope

joy

peace

Love

noel

Marbled Greeting Cookies

Chocolate-Covered Praline Chews (p. 70)
Peppermint Fudge Truffles
Cherry Pistachio Bark

Enchanting Candy

★ *When holiday guests discover these rich, decadent confections on your Christmas treat tray, you'll want to be ready with refills!* ★

Peppermint Fudge Truffles

These candy-coated bites always stand out among my holiday goodies. No one can resist the creamy fudge and refreshing peppermint flavor. ~Tracy Travers, Fairhaven, Massachusetts

  1 cup milk chocolate chips
  1 can (16 ounces) chocolate frosting
1-1/2 cups peppermint crunch baking chips, *divided*
  1/2 cup chopped walnuts *or* pecans
  1/8 teaspoon peppermint extract

1. In a microwave-safe bowl, melt milk chocolate chips; stir until smooth. Stir in the frosting, 1/2 cup peppermint chips, walnuts and extract. Cover and chill for 30 minutes or until firm enough to form into balls.

2. Coarsely chop remaining peppermint chips. Shape chocolate mixture into 1-in. balls; roll in chopped chips. Store in an airtight container in the refrigerator. **Yield:** 4 dozen.

Editor's Note: This recipe was tested with Andes Peppermint Crunch Baking Chips.

Cherry Pistachio Bark

Dotted with red cherry bits, these diamond-shaped pieces are lovely on a tray. Plus, they come together quickly with four ingredients. ~Beth Jenkins-Horsley, Belmont, North Carolina

  2 packages (10 to 12 ounces *each*) vanilla *or* white chips
  12 ounces white candy coating, chopped
1-1/4 cups dried cherries, chopped
1-1/4 cups pistachios, chopped

1. Line a 15-in. x 10-in. x 1-in. pan with foil; set aside. In a microwave-safe bowl, melt chips and candy coating; stir until smooth. Stir in the cherries and pistachios. Spread into prepared pan. Refrigerate for 20 minutes.

2. Using a sharp knife, score the surface of the candy, making diamond shapes about 1/8 in. deep. Refrigerate 40 minutes longer or until set. Cut along the scored lines into diamonds. Store candy in an airtight container in the refrigerator. **Yield:** 3 pounds.

Caramel-Nut Candy Bars

As a busy mother of six, I welcome any Christmas recipe that's quick, easy and family pleasing. These Snickers-like bars fit that description perfectly! ~Sheralyn Ylioja, Lethbridge, Alberta

1-1/2 teaspoons plus 1/4 cup butter, softened, *divided*
  2 packages (11-1/2 ounces *each*) milk chocolate chips
  1/4 cup shortening
  1 package (14 ounces) caramels
  5 teaspoons water
  1 cup chopped pecans

1. Line a 13-in. x 9-in. x 2-in. pan with foil and grease the foil with 1-1/2 teaspoons butter; set aside. In a large microwave-safe bowl, melt chocolate chips and shortening; stir until smooth. Spread half of the mixture into prepared pan. Refrigerate for 15 minutes or until firm. Set remaining chocolate mixture aside.

2. In another large microwave-safe bowl, heat the caramels, water and remaining butter at 70% power for 2 minutes; stir. Microwave in 10- to 20-second intervals until melted; stir until smooth. Stir in pecans. Spread over chocolate layer.

3. Heat reserved chocolate mixture if necessary to achieve spreading consistency; spread over caramel layer. Cover and refrigerate for 1 hour or until firm.

4. Using foil, lift candy out of pan. Gently peel off foil; cut candy into 1-1/2-in. x 1-in. bars. Store in the refrigerator. **Yield:** 2-1/4 pounds.

Editor's Note: This recipe was tested in a 1,100-watt microwave.

Caramel-Nut Candy Bars

Popcorn Delight

Popcorn Delight

Whenever I take this sweet mix somewhere, I bring copies of the recipe because people always ask for it. Once you start munching, it's hard to stop! ~Cheryl Bull, Blue Grass, Iowa

    14 cups popped popcorn
    2 cups salted peanuts
    2 cups crisp rice cereal
    2 cups miniature marshmallows
    1 pound white candy coating, chopped
    3 tablespoons creamy peanut butter

1. In a large bowl, combine the popcorn, peanuts, cereal and marshmallows. In a microwave-safe bowl, melt candy coating and peanut butter; stir until smooth. Pour over popcorn mixture and toss to coat.

2. Spread onto waxed paper-lined baking sheets; refrigerate for 15 minutes or until set. Break into pieces. Store in an airtight container in the refrigerator. **Yield:** about 6 quarts.

Pineapple Fudge

Pineapple may seem like a strange ingredient for your Christmas fudge, but this light-colored version is a really yummy, refreshing change of pace from the usual chocolate variety. Try the recipe and see for yourself! ~Ruth McNally, Rozet, Wyoming

    3 tablespoons butter, softened, *divided*
    3 cups sugar
    1 can (16 ounces) crushed pineapple, drained
  1/2 cup heavy whipping cream
    1 tablespoon light corn syrup
  1/2 teaspoon vanilla extract

    1 cup chopped nuts
    1 to 2 drops yellow food coloring

1. Line an 8-in. square dish with foil. Using 1 tablespo[on] butter, grease the foil and the sides of a heavy large saucepa[n]. Add the sugar, pineapple, cream and corn syrup to th[e] saucepan. Cook and stir over medium heat until a candy ther[mometer reads 234° (soft-ball stage).

2. Remove from the heat; add remaining butter (do not stir) Cool to 125°. Add vanilla; stir until combined. Beat with [a] wooden spoon until mixture is thickened and lighter in co[l]or, about 5 minutes.

3. Stir in nuts and food coloring. Spread into prepared pa[n;] let stand until firm. Using foil, lift fudge out of pan; cut in[to] 1-in. squares. Store in an airtight container in the refriger[a]tor. **Yield:** 2-1/4 pounds.

Editor's Note: We recommend that you test your cand[y] thermometer before each use by bringing water to a bo[il;] the thermometer should read 212°. Adjust your recipe tem[]perature up or down based on your test.

Chocolate-Covered Praline Chews

(Pictured on page 68)

The contrasting milk chocolate and white candy coating mak[e] these chewy treats eye-catching...and they taste as good as the[y] look. ~Christina Mitchell, Haughton, Louisian[a]

    1 cup sugar
    1 cup light corn syrup
Dash salt
  1/4 cup butter, cubed
    2 teaspoons milk
    2 cups pecan halves
  1/2 teaspoon vanilla extract
    6 ounces white candy coating
    6 ounces milk chocolate candy coating

1. In a heavy saucepan, combine the sugar, corn syrup an[d] salt. Bring to a boil over medium heat; cook until a candy ther[mometer reads 245° (firm-ball stage), stirring occasional[ly] Gradually stir in the butter, milk and pecans. Continu[e] cooking until temperature returns to 245°.

2. Remove from the heat; stir in vanilla. Immediately dro[p] by tablespoonfuls onto greased baking sheets. Cool.

3. In a microwave-safe bowl, melt white candy coating. Di[p] candies halfway into coating and allow excess to drip off. Plac[e] on waxed paper-lined baking sheets; refrigerate for 15 min[]utes or until set. Melt milk chocolate coating; dip other ha[lf] of each candy and allow excess to drip off. Return to bakin[g] sheets; refrigerate until set. **Yield:** about 3 dozen.

Editor's Note: We recommend that you test your cand[y] thermometer before each use by bringing water to a bo[il;] the thermometer should read 212°. Adjust your recipe tem[]perature up or down based on your test.

Festive Anise Hard Candy

Anyone who likes the flavor of anise is sure to enjoy these five-ingredient candies. The bright red color makes them perfect for the holiday season. ~Irma Lien, Beaverton, Oregon

2 cups sugar
1 cup water
1 cup light corn syrup
2 to 3 teaspoons anise extract *or* 1 teaspoon anise oil
8 to 10 drops red food coloring

1. In a large heavy saucepan, combine the sugar, water and corn syrup. Bring to a boil over medium heat, stirring occasionally. Cover and cook for 3 minutes or until sugar is dissolved. Uncover; cook over medium heat, without stirring, until a candy thermometer reads 300° (hard-crack stage).

2. Remove the mixture from the heat; stir in the anise extract and red food coloring (if you are using anise oil, keep your face away from the mixture as the aroma will be very strong). Pour the mixture into a buttered 13-in. x 9-in. x 2-in. pan. When cooled slightly but not hardened, cut candy into 1-in. squares. Cool completely. Store in an airtight container. **Yield:** about 1 pound.

Editor's Note: We recommend that you test your candy thermometer before each use by bringing water to a boil; the thermometer should read 212°. Adjust your recipe temperature up or down based on your test.

Raspberry Rocky Road Fudge

With raspberry-flavored chips and marshmallows, these irresistible squares will thrill any sweet tooth. Plenty of peanuts add a nice crunch, too. ~Tracie Calkin, Casper, Wyoming

1-1/2 teaspoons plus 1/2 cup butter, softened, *divided*
2 cups sugar
12 large marshmallows
1 can (5 ounces) evaporated milk
1/4 teaspoon salt
1 package (12 ounces) semisweet chocolate chips, *divided*
1 cup raspberry chocolate chips
3/4 cup creamy peanut butter
1 teaspoon vanilla extract
1-2/3 cups salted peanuts, crushed

1. Line a 13-in. x 9-in. x 2-in. pan with foil and butter the foil with 1-1/2 teaspoons butter; set aside. In a large saucepan, combine the sugar, marshmallows, milk, salt and remaining butter. Bring to a boil over medium heat, stirring constantly. Cook and stir until smooth.

2. Remove from the heat. Stir in the semisweet chocolate chips, raspberry chocolate chips, peanut butter and vanilla until smooth. Fold in peanuts. Spread into prepared pan. Refrigerate for 2 hours or until set.

3. Using the foil, lift the fudge out of the pan; cut into 1-in. squares. Store in an airtight container in the refrigerator. **Yield:** about 3-1/2 pounds.

Coconut Almond Candies

I love Christmas candy, and these simple but special chocolates are among my favorites. They're easy to assemble in paper-lined muffin cups. ~Donald Brownell, Mt. Crawford, Virginia

2 cups flaked coconut, chopped
3 tablespoons sweetened condensed milk
3 tablespoons confectioners' sugar
2 teaspoons butter, softened
1 package (12 ounces) semisweet chocolate chips, *divided*
8 ounces white candy coating
1 tablespoon shortening
1 package (2-1/4 ounces) unblanched almonds

1. In a large mixing bowl, beat the coconut, milk, confectioners' sugar and butter until blended (mixture will be sticky); set aside.

2. In a microwave-safe bowl, melt chocolate chips, candy coating and shortening; stir until smooth. Spoon about 1/2 teaspoon chocolate mixture into 42 paper-lined miniature muffin cups.

3. Shape 1/2 teaspoonfuls of coconut mixture into balls; gently press into chocolate. Top each with an almond. Spoon 1 teaspoon chocolate mixture over each. Let stand until set. Store in an airtight container. **Yield:** 3-1/2 dozen.

Coconut Almond Candies

Give Rise to the
Merriest Bread Ever!

WITH CHEEKS like roses and a nose like a cherry, you may want to serve this loaf with a bowlful of jelly!

From Vicki Melies, the colorful Santa Claus bread is sure to be the talk of your Christmas table. "A friend of mine shared this fun idea," Vicki relates from Glenwood, Iowa. "She made it with purchased frozen dough, and I use a family recipe." (To use frozen dough, see the tip box at bottom right.)

After shaping the dough into a cute Kris Kringle, Vicki brushes on a tinted egg wash for the red coloring and adds raisin eyes. "The finished loaf looks complicated, but it's actually simple to create," she assures.

Tender and golden, the bread is also entirely edible. But it's so adorable, you'll want to display it a while first!

Golden Santa Bread

    4 to 4-1/2 cups bread flour
    1/2 cup sugar
    2 packages (1/4 ounce *each*) active dry yeast
1-1/2 teaspoons salt
    1/2 cup milk
    1/4 cup water
    1/4 cup butter, cubed
        2 eggs
        2 raisins
        2 egg yolks
        2 to 3 drops red food coloring

In a large mixing bowl, combine 2 cups flour, sugar, yeast and salt. In a small saucepan, heat the milk, water and butter to 120°-130°. Add to dry ingredients; beat just until moistened. Beat in the eggs until smooth. Stir in enough remaining flour to form a stiff dough.

Turn onto a floured surface; knead until smooth and elastic, about 6-8 minutes. Place in a greased bowl, turning once to grease top. Cover and let rise in a warm place until doubled, about 1 hour.

Punch dough down. Turn onto a lightly floured surface; divide into two portions, one slightly larger than the other. Shape the larger portion into an elongated triangle with rounded corners for Santa's head and hat. Divide the smaller portion in half. Shape and flatten one half into a beard. Using scissors or a pizza cutter, cut into strips to within 1 in. of top. Position on Santa's face; twist and curl strips if desired.

Use the remaining dough for the mustache, nose, hat pom-pom and brim. Shape a portion of dough into a mustache; flatten and cut the ends into small strips with scissors. Place above beard. Place a small ball above mustache for nose. Fold tip of hat over and add another ball for pom-pom. Roll out a narrow piece of dough to create a hat brim; position under hat.

With a scissors, cut two slits for eyes; insert raisins into slits. In separate small bowls, beat each egg yolk. Add red food coloring to one yolk; carefully brush over hat, nose and cheeks. Brush plain yolk over remaining dough.

Cover loosely with foil. Bake at 350° for 15 minutes. Uncover; bake 10-12 minutes longer or until golden brown. Cool on a wire rack. **Yield:** 1 loaf.

Shaping Santa

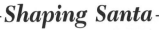

Fig. 1: On a lightly floured surface, shape the larger portion of bread dough into an elongated triangle with rounded corners for Santa's head and hat.

Fig. 2: Shape and flatten half of the smaller portion of dough into a beard. Using a scissors or pizza cutter, cut the beard into strips to within 1 in. of the top of the beard.

Fig. 3: Carefully pick up the cut beard piece with both hands and position the beard on the bottom of Santa's face.

Fig. 4: If desired, twist the cut strips in the beard and slightly curl up the ends of the strips to shape the beard.

Fig. 5: Add red food coloring to one beaten egg yolk and carefully brush the tinted red yolk over the hat, nose and cheeks.

Make Santa Even Speedier

Want to save time when making the Golden Santa Bread? Instead of stirring up homemade dough, start with 2 loaves of purchased frozen bread dough and turn them onto a lightly floured surface. Take a small portion of one loaf and add it to the other loaf, making it slightly larger. Then begin shaping the Santa with the dough following the instructions.

Seasonal Crafts

Make merry this Christmas with fun and easy holiday handcrafts—from festive family keepsakes to heartwarming gifts.

Star Runner Makes A Plain Table Shine

IN A TWINKLING, this quilted covering can turn an everyday table into a seasonal showpiece. "This appliqued project is easy enough for beginners," notes Mary Cain, Sun Prairie, Wisconsin.

MATERIALS NEEDED:
Patterns at bottom right
Paper-backed fusible web
Tracing paper and pencil
44-inch-wide 100% cotton fabrics—1/8 yard each of eight
 different coordinating print fabrics for pieced squares,
 1/8 yard of coordinating small print for inner border,
 1/4 yard of dark print for outer border, 1/4 yard of dark
 print for binding, 1/6 yard of small gold print for star
 appliques and 5/8 yard for backing
20-inch x 44-inch piece of lightweight quilt batting
All-purpose thread—neutral or colors to match fabrics
Rayon or decorative thread in color to coordinate with
 star applique fabric
Tear-away stabilizer
Quilter's marking pen or pencil (optional)
Quilter's ruler
Rotary cutting tools (optional)
Standard sewing supplies

FINISHED SIZE: Runner is about 17 inches wide x 41 inches long.

DIRECTIONS:
CUTTING: Either use quilter's marking pen or pencil to mark the fabrics before cutting them with a scissors or use rotary cutting tools to cut the pieces as directed in the instructions that follow. Cut strips crosswise from selvage to selvage.

Trim each of the eight different fabrics for squares into 4-inch-wide strips. From each strip, cut four 4-inch squares, creating a total of thirty-two 4-inch squares.

From the fabric for the inner border, cut two 1-inch-wide x 11-inch-long strips and two 1-inch-wide x 37-inch-long strips.

From the fabric for the outer border, cut two 37-inch-long x 3-inch-wide strips and two 3-inch-wide x 17-inch-long strips.

From binding fabric, cut three 2-1/4-inch-wide strips.

PIECING: Do all stitching with right sides of fabrics together, edges even, matching or neutral thread and an accurate 1/4-inch seam. Press seams as directed.

Lay out 30 of the 4-inch squares randomly in three rows with 10 squares in each row (there will be two extra squares).

Sew the blocks in each row together in planned order. Press seams in each row in opposite directions. Sew the rows together. Press seams in opposite directions.

APPLIQUES: Trace the star patterns separately onto tracing paper with pencil.

Trace each star twice onto paper side of fusible web, leaving at least 1/2 inch between shapes. Cut shapes apart, leaving a margin of paper around each.

Fuse stars onto wrong side of gold applique fabric following manufacturer's instructions. When cool, cut out stars along outline of patterns. Remove paper backing.

Referring to photo at left for placement, fuse stars to right side of pieced runner. Place tear-away stabilizer behind stars. Using rayon or decorative thread, blanket-stitch around each star. Bring all loose threads to the back and secure. Remove stabilizer.

INNER BORDER: Sew short inner border strips to opposite short edges of pieced top. Press seam toward inner border.

In the same way, sew the long inner border strips to the opposite long edges of the pieced top. Press as before.

OUTER BORDER: Sew long outer border strips to opposite long edges of the inner border. Press seam toward outer border.

In the same way, sew the short outer border strips to the opposite short edges of the inner border. Press as before.

QUILTING: Place backing fabric wrong side up on a flat surface. Center batting on top of backing. Center pieced runner on top of batting. Smooth out all wrinkles. Baste layers together as needed to hold. Quilt as desired.

Trim excess batting and backing even with outer edges.

BINDING: Sew narrow ends of binding strips together diagonally to make one long strip. Trim one short end of binding strip diagonally and press 1/4 inch to wrong side.

Fold and press binding strip in half lengthwise with wrong sides facing. Sew binding to front of runner with a 1/4-inch seam, mitering corners and overlapping ends. Trim excess binding. Fold binding to back of runner, encasing raw edges and mitering corners.

With matching or neutral thread, either sew binding in place using a long zigzag stitch or hand-sew fold of binding to backing. Remove basting. ❁

STAR RUNNER

LARGE STAR
Trace 1—tracing paper
Cut 2—fused gold print

MEDIUM STAR
Trace 1—tracing paper
Cut 2—fused gold print

SMALL STAR
Trace 1—tracing paper
Cut 2—fused gold print

Joyful Candles Spell Out Holiday Spirit

IN A WORD, these Noel votives are letter-perfect! Mary Ayres of Boyce, Virginia made the plain glass candle holders festive for Christmas using basic paper-crafting supplies.

MATERIALS NEEDED:

Three clear glass votive holders with straight sides
Three coordinating patterned scrapbook papers
   (Mary used Foof-a-la Mod Sparklers papers)
Circle punches or circle templates—1-3/8-inch and
   1-inch
1/16-inch circle punch
3/8-inch-wide ribbon—10-inch length each of three
   different coordinating colors
Card stock—blue, lime green, purple, red, turquoise and
   white
Black fine-line permanent marker
Round mini brads—one each of blue, lime green and
   purple
Glue (Mary used Beacon Adhesives Zip-Dry Glue)
Ruler
Scissors
Computer and printer (optional)

FINISHED SIZE: Each votive holder measures about 2 inches wide x 2-3/4 inches high.

DIRECTIONS:

From each of the three patterned scrapbook papers, cut a rec-tangular piece to fit around the votive holders.

Use ruler and marker to draw a line 1/8-inch from the long edges on each of the rectangles.

Punch or cut a 1-3/8-inch circle from blue, red and purple card stock.

Use computer or marker to print or write "J" on the lime green card stock, "O" on the white card stock and "Y" on the turquoise card stock.

With the letters centered, punch or cut out the card stock letters using the 1-inch circle punch or template.

Use marker to draw a line about 1/8 inch from the outer edge of each of the letter circles.

Glue the letter circles to the larger circles as shown in the photo, leaving space above the letters for brads. Let dry.

Use 1/16-inch circle punch to punch a hole through the top of each large circle. Through each patterned paper rectan-gle, punch a 1/16-inch hole that is centered along one long edge and about 3/8 inch from the long edge.

Insert a brad through punched hole of large circle and then through the hole on one of the patterned paper rectan-gles. Open and bend ends of brad flat on back of paper. Posi-tion the brad ends so they are vertical, allowing the paper to wrap smoothly around the votive holder. Repeat with each re-maining circle and paper rectangle.

Wrap and glue a patterned paper rectangle right side up around each votive holder. Let dry.

Wrap a ribbon piece around the bottom of a votive holder. Tie the ends in a knot in front under the letter. Use scissors to trim ends as desired. Repeat using the remaining ribbons and holders.

Angle the letters on each votive and glue to secure. ❋

Snuggly Santa Doll Makes Kids Merry

EYES will be twinkling when they spy this knit St. Nick under the tree. "The doll takes just 2 or 3 evenings to complete," notes Margie Wilkins of Falls Church, Virginia.

MATERIALS NEEDED:

Worsted-weight yarn—3-ounce skein of red and small amount each of black, blue, gold, green, peach and white
White mohair yarn—small amount for beard and hair
Size 6 (4mm) knitting needles
Two stitch holders
Yarn or tapestry needle
Size G (4.25mm) crochet hook
Scissors

STITCH USED: Santa doll is worked in St st.
Row 1: K across row (RS)
Row 2: P across row (WS)
Repeat Rows 1 and 2.

NOTE: All inc and dec sts are worked on K (RS) rows.

GAUGE: Working in St st: 5 sts and 6 rows = 1 inches. Slight variation in gauge will change finished sit a bit.

FINISHED SIZE: Santa doll measures about 12 inches wide x 20 inches high.

DIRECTIONS:

LEG (make two): With black, cast on 18 sts.
Rows 1-10: Work in St st. Change to white at end of Row 10: 18 sts.
Rows 11-14: Work in St st. Change to red at end of Row 14: 18 sts.
Rows 15-27: Work in St st. Place sts on stitch holder at end of Row 27: 18 sts.
Repeat to make second leg.
LOWER BODY: With red and RS facing, pick up and k sts on both stitch holders: 36 sts.
Row 1 (WS): P across row: 36 sts.
Row 2 (RS): K 2, inc 1, k 9, inc 1, k 14, inc 1, k 9, inc 1, k 2: 40 sts.
Row 3: P across row: 40 sts.
Row 4: K 2, inc 1, k 10, inc 1, k 16, inc 1, k 10, inc 1, k 2: 44 sts.
Row 5: P across row: 44 sts.
Row 6: K 2, inc 1, k 11, inc 1, k 18, inc 1, k 11, inc 1, k 2: 48 sts.
Row 7: P across row: 48 sts.
Row 8: K 2, inc 1, k 12, inc 1, k 20, inc 1, k 12, inc 1, k 2: 52 sts.
Row 9: P across row: 52 sts.
Row 10: K 2, inc 1, k 13, inc 1, k 22, inc 1, k 13, inc 1, k 2: 56 sts.

Row 11: P across row: 56 sts.
Row 12: K across row: 56 sts.
Row 13: P across row: 56 sts. Drop red.
BELT: Row 1: With black, k 25, with gold, k 6, with black, k 25: 56 sts.
Row 2: With black, p 25, with gold, p 2, with black, p 2, with gold, p 2, with black, p 25: 56 sts.
Row 3: With black, k 25, with gold, k 2, with black, k 2, with gold, k 2, with black, k 25: 56 sts.
Row 4: With black, p 25, with gold, p 6, with black, k 25: 56 sts. Fasten off gold and black.
UPPER BODY: Row 1: With red, k across row: 56 sts.
Row 2: P across row: 56 sts.
Rows 3-4: Repeat Rows 1 and 2: 56 sts.
Row 5: K 2, k2tog, k 10, k2tog, k 24, k2tog, k 10, k2tog, k 2: 52 sts.
Row 6: P across row: 52 sts.
Row 7: K across row: 52 sts.
Row 8: P across row: 52 sts.
Row 9: K 2, k2tog, k 10, k2tog, k 20, k2tog, k 10, k2tog, k 2: 48 sts.
Row 10: P across row: 48 sts.
Row 11: K across row: 48 sts.

(Continued on next page)

Row 12: P across row: 48 sts.

Row 13: K 2, k2tog, k 10, k2tog, k 16, k2tog, k 10, k2tog, k 2: 44 sts.

Row 14: P across row: 44 sts.

Row 15: K across row: 44 sts.

Row 16: P across row: 44 sts. Fasten off red.

Row 17: With white, k across row: 44 sts.

Row 18: P across row: 44 sts.

Row 19: K across row: 44 sts.

Row 20: P across row: 44 sts. Fasten off white.

HEAD: Row 1: With peach, k across row: 44 sts.

Row 2: P across row: 44 sts.

Rows 3-20: Repeat Head Rows 1 and 2: 44 sts.

Row 21: [K 2, k2tog] across row: 33 sts.

Row 22: P across row: 33 sts.

Row 23: [K 1, k2tog] across row: 22 sts.

Row 24: P across row: 22 sts.

Row 25: [K2tog] across row: 11 sts. Cut yarn, leaving a 16-inch tail of yarn.

Thread yarn through sts on needle. Draw sts up tightly. Thread yarn on yarn or tapestry needle. Sew straight edges of head together and stuff head firmly. Gather sts around first row of peach. Pull yarn tight and fasten off to form neck.

With right sides together and with matching yarn, sew inner seams of each leg to crotch. Turn each leg right side out. Stuff each leg firmly.

With matching yarn, sew straight edges of body together, stuffing the body firmly as you sew.

With red yarn, stitch across the top of each leg, stitching from front to back to flatten the top of each leg so Santa doll will sit.

FACE: Thread yarn or tapestry needle with blue yarn. Knot ends together.

Insert needle through back of Santa's head and out on front about 2-1/2 inches from top of head. Make a short horizontal stitch for first eye. Run needle to side to make second horizontal stitch for second eye. Insert needle through to back of head and fasten off yarn.

NOSE: Starting with a 12-inch tail of peach yarn, ch 20. Fasten off, leaving a 12-inch tail of yarn.

Thread yarn ends on yarn or tapestry needle. Wind the chain and sew it in a circle. Sew nose to front of Santa's head. Insert needle to back of Santa's head and fasten off.

ARM (make two): With red, cast on 16 sts.

Rows 1-12: Work in St st: 16 sts. Fasten off red at end of Row 12.

Rows 13-16: With white, work in St st: 16 sts. Fasten off white at end of Row 16.

Rows 17-24: With green, work in St st: 16 sts.

Row 25: [K2tog] across row: 8 sts. Fasten off, leaving a 10-inch tail of yarn.

Thread yarn through sts on needle. Draw up sts tightly.

With matching yarn and right sides facing, sew straight edges of arm together. Turn right side out. Stuff arm.

Repeat to make second arm.

With matching yarn, sew arms to opposite sides of body.

HAT: With white, cast on 44 sts.

Rows 1-4: Work in St st: 44 sts. Fasten off white at end of Row 4.

Rows 5-6: With red, work in St st: 44 sts.

Row 7: K 1, k2tog, k across to last 3 sts, k2tog, k 1.

Row 8: P across row.

Rows 9-43: Repeat Hat Rows 7 and 8 until 8 sts remain, ending with a k row. Fasten off red at end of last row.

Row 44: With white, p across row: 8 sts.

Rows 45-49: Work in St st: 8 sts.

Row 50: [K2tog] across row: 4 sts. Fasten off, leaving a tail of yarn. Thread yarn through sts on needle. Draw up sts tightly. With matching yarn, sew straight edges of white together, stuffing as you sew.

With matching yarn, sew straight edges of hat together.

Place hat on Santa's head with seam in back. Pull hat down to neck in back. With white yarn, sew hat to Santa's head, stitching in center of white band so white band rolls up and covers the stitching.

HAIR AND BEARD: Thread yarn or tapestry needle with a double strand of mohair yarn.

For hair, make small overlapping knotted loop stitches along lower edge of hat. Secure each loop with an anchor stitch. See Fig. 1 below for stitch illustration.

In the same way, make three rows of loop stitches across Santa's face for beard. ❀

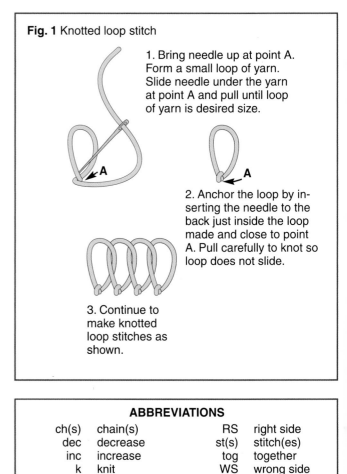

Fig. 1 Knotted loop stitch

1. Bring needle up at point A. Form a small loop of yarn. Slide needle under the yarn at point A and pull until loop of yarn is desired size.

2. Anchor the loop by inserting the needle to the back just inside the loop made and close to point A. Pull carefully to knot so loop does not slide.

3. Continue to make knotted loop stitches as shown.

ABBREVIATIONS

ch(s)	chain(s)	RS	right side
dec	decrease	st(s)	stitch(es)
inc	increase	tog	together
k	knit	WS	wrong side
p	purl		

[ ] Instructions within bracket are repeated as directed.

Jars Put a Festive Label on Christmas

LIFT THE LID on this idea from Loretta Mateik, and you'll find fun wrappers that are perfect for jam, salsa or other gifts from the kitchen. "I used jelly jars, but this project will work with jars of other sizes, too," she writes from Petaluma, California.

MATERIALS NEEDED (for all):
Three glass jars with lids and bands (Loretta used jelly jars)
Card stock—one sheet each of a print and a coordinating solid for each jar wrapper, plus scraps each of green, gold and white solid
Tree, snowflake and star punches (optional)
Coordinating chalk or colored pencils
Black fine-line marker
14-inch length of coordinating ribbon or length needed to tie around jar
Two metal eyelets and eyelet setting tools
Pop-ups or glue dots
Paper glue
Double-stick tape
Measuring tape
Scissors
Computer and printer (optional)

FINISHED SIZE: Each jelly jar shown in photo measures about 2-5/8 inches wide x 4 inches high.

DIRECTIONS:
Measure around jar and add 1 inch to that measurement. Measure the height of jar from just below the rim to about 3/8 inch from the bottom. Cut a rectangular piece of solid card stock equal to these measurements.

Cut a piece of patterned card stock that has the same length as the solid piece but is about 1/4 inch narrower.

Glue the patterned piece of card stock to the solid piece, leaving a margin of solid paper showing along both long edges.

Using double-stick tape, adhere layered card stock to outside of jar. Overlap the narrow ends and use double-stick tape to secure them.

Using a computer or marker, write a greeting on paper and cut it in a circle to fit on jar lid. Glue circle to lid.

FINISHING: Tree jar: Wrap jar with length of coordinating ribbon. Knot ribbon in back of jar.

Cut a tree shape from green solid card stock using a scissors or punch.

Attach the tree to the ribbon on front of jar using a pop-up or glue dot.

Star jar: Cut a star shape from gold solid card stock using a scissors or punch.

Use marker to write contents of jar on star.

Rub edges of star with chalk or colored pencil to shade.

Attach eyelets to opposite sides of star and thread ribbon through the eyelets. Wrap the ribbon around the jar and knot the ends in back.

Snowflake jar: Wrap jar with length of coordinating ribbon. Knot ribbon in back of jar.

Cut a snowflake shape from white solid card stock using a scissors or punch.

Use marker to write contents of jar on snowflake.

Rub edges of snowflake with chalk or colored pencil to shade.

Attach snowflake to ribbon on front of jar using a pop-up or glue dot. ❈

Cardigan Idea Makes A Plain Shirt Merry

WEAR your creativity on your sleeve with this country-style cardigan from Elaine Pfeifer of Norfolk, Nebraska. She appliqued a plain red sweatshirt to fashion this Christmasy cover-up.

MATERIALS NEEDED:

Purchased sweatshirt—red or desired color

Eight 5-inch squares of coordinating 100% cotton or cotton-blend fabrics for background of appliques (Elaine used four coordinating check and plaid fabrics)

100% cotton or cotton-blend fabrics—scraps each of black solid, red solid flannel, green solid, green mottled print, tan solid and white-on-white print for appliques

Paper-backed fusible web

Pencil

All-purpose thread to match sweatshirt and fabrics

Quilter's ruler (optional)

Rotary cutter and mat (optional)

Twenty-one two-hole or four-hole buttons in assorted sizes and coordinating colors

Pearl cotton—black and white

Dimensional craft/fabric paint—black and orange

Black fine-line permanent marker

Standard sewing supplies

FINISHED SIZE: Finished size will vary depending on the size of the sweatshirt. Each appliqued square is 4 inches wide x 4 inches high.

DIRECTIONS:

Wash and dry the sweatshirt following the manufacturer's instructions.

Carefully cut off ribbing from each sleeve and from the bottom of the sweatshirt.

Measure sweatshirt from each underarm to bottom edge. Trim the bottom of the sweatshirt evenly if needed.

Measure your desired sleeve length and trim excess from the end of sleeves if needed. If the width of the sleeve is too big, taper the sleeve up to the underarm.

Cut up the center front of the sweatshirt from the bottom to the top to create a cardigan.

Turn the bottom edge of each sleeve 1/2 inch to the wrong side. Machine-sew hem in place with matching thread and a

(Continued on page 82)

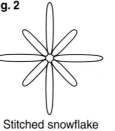

Fig. 1	**Fig. 2**
Blanket stitch	Stitched snowflake

SMALL HEART
Trace 1—paper-backed
fusible web
Cut 1—fused black
solid

BOW TIE
Trace 2—paper-
backed fusible web
Cut 1—fused black
solid
Cut 1—fused red
solid flannel

LARGE HEART
Trace 1—paper-backed fusible web
Cut 1—fused red solid

SNOWMAN
Trace 2—
paper-backed
fusible web
Cut 2—fused
white-on-white
print

MITTENS
Trace 4, reversing 2—paper-
backed fusible web
Cut 1 each mitten—fused black
solid
Cut 1 each mitten—fused red
solid flannel

STAR
Trace 1—paper-backed
fusible web
Cut 1—fused tan solid

TREE
Trace 2—paper-backed fusible web
Cut 1—fused green solid
Cut 1—fused green mottled print

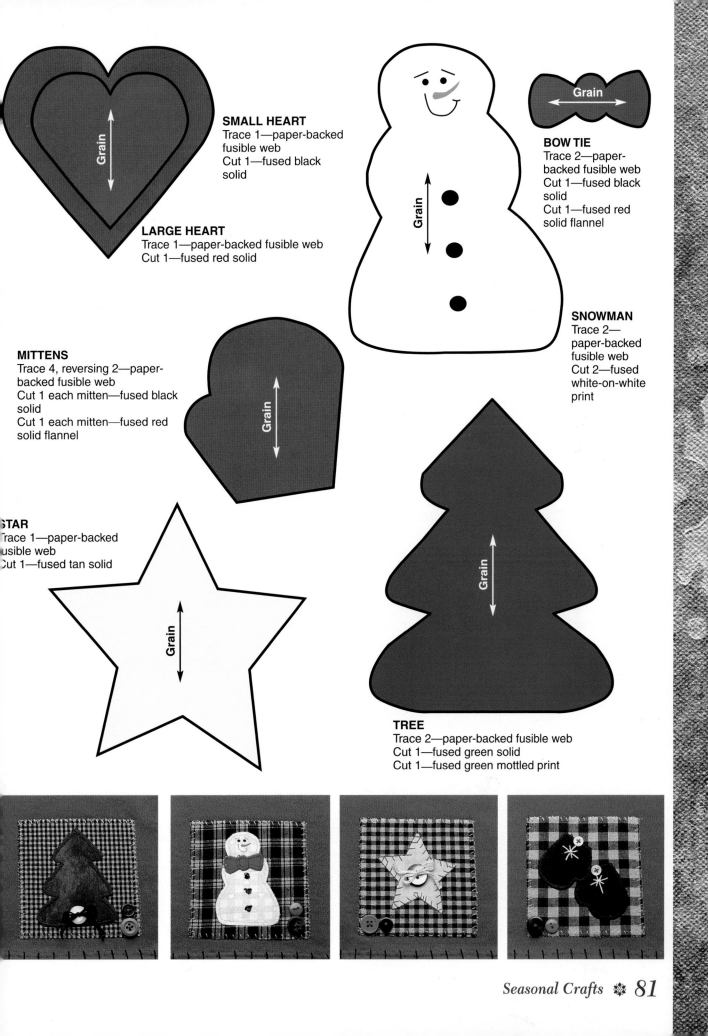

Seasonal Crafts ❋ *81*

wide zigzag or long blanket stitch.

In the same way, hem the bottom edge of the sweatshirt and then the left and right front edges of the sweatshirt.

Thread hand-sewing needle with black pearl cotton and blanket-stitch around each hem. See Fig. 1 on page 80 for stitch illustration.

APPLIQUES: Fuse a slightly smaller piece of paper-backed fusible web to the wrong side of each fabric square for the background of the appliques. Trim each to an accurate 4-inch square. Do not remove paper backing.

Trace patterns on page 80 onto paper side of fusible web as directed on patterns, leaving at least 1/2 inch between the shapes. Cut shapes apart, leaving a margin of paper around each. Fuse shapes to wrong side of fabrics as directed.

Cut out shapes, cutting along pattern lines.

Remove paper backing and position shapes on fused squares of fabric. Fuse shapes to fabric squares.

Applique around shapes with matching thread and a narrow satin stitch. Pull threads to back and fasten off loose ends.

Thread hand-sewing needle with white pearl cotton and stitch a snowflake on each appliqued mitten. See Fig. 2 for stitch illustration.

Remove paper backing from appliqued squares. Position the squares evenly spaced along bottom edge of sweatshirt. Fuse the squares in place.

Machine-sew around each square with matching thread and a wide zigzag or long blanket stitch.

Using black or white pearl cotton and leaving thread ends on the front, sew a contrasting button to the bottom of each Christmas tree. Tie ends of pearl cotton in a small bow.

Hand-sew remaining buttons where shown.

Use orange dimensional craft/fabric paint to add a small orange triangle to each snowman for nose.

Use black dimensional craft/fabric paint to add two tiny dots for eyes and to add three small dots for coal buttons on each snowman.

Use black marker to add eyebrows and a mouth to each snowman. ❄

Folksy Santas Start With Simple Items

ALL THROUGH her Corning, New York house, Irene Wegener finds objects to use for crafting. "I painted these Santa faces on an old shoehorn and two table knives," she says. "They make unusual ornaments and always get noticed."

MATERIALS NEEDED (for all):
White spray primer
Water basin
Paper towels
Foam plate or palette
Acrylic craft paints (Irene used Delta Ceramcoat paints)—Antique Gold, Antique White, Black, Black Cherry, Brown Velvet, Fleshtone and Rouge
Paintbrushes—small flat, small angle brush and liner
Toothpick
Glue gun and glue stick
Gloss spray sealer
Pencil
Ruler

MATERIALS NEEDED (for shoehorn):
Shoehorn
1-1/2-inch-wide x 10-inch-long torn strip of dark green plaid fabric for hanger
1/2-inch-high wooden star
Black fine-line permanent marker

MATERIALS NEEDED (for both knives):
Dinner knife
Butter knife
Drill with 1/8-inch bit
Two 12-inch lengths of 1/8-inch-wide green satin ribbon for hangers
Two 2-inch lengths of tiny artificial berry garland

FINISHED SIZE: Finished size will vary depending on size of shoehorn and knives used. Irene used a standard shoehorn, dinner knife and butter knife.

DIRECTIONS:

Spray all sides of shoehorn and knives with two coats of white primer following manufacturer's instructions. Let dry.

Keep paper towels and a container of water handy to clean paintbrushes. Place small amounts of paint as needed onto foam plate or palette. Add coats of paint as needed for complete coverage. Let paint dry after every application. Refer to photo on page 82 as a guide while painting as directed in the instructions that follow.

SHOEHORN: Bend top of shoehorn as shown in photo.

Painted design shown in the photo is done on the side of the shoehorn that curves outward.

Use pencil to draw a 3/8-inch-wide band across the center of the shoehorn for the trim of hat. Also use pencil to draw the outline of the face as shown in photo.

Use flat brush and Black Cherry to paint hat on front and back of shoehorn.

Use flat brush and Antique Gold to paint hat trim and to paint all sides of wooden star.

Use flat brush and Fleshtone to paint Santa's face.

Use flat brush and Antique White to paint remainder of the front of shoehorn for beard. Also paint the remainder of the back of shoehorn.

Use flat brush and Black to shade lower edge of hat.

Use flat brush and Brown Velvet to shade outer edge of beard. With a nearly dry brush, add some vertical streaks to the beard.

Dip toothpick into Black and add two small dots for eyes.

Use liner and Antique White to add eyebrows.

Dip toothpick into Antique White and add a tiny dot to each eye for highlight.

Dip flat brush into Rouge and wipe off excess paint onto paper towel. With a nearly dry brush and a circular motion, add cheeks to Santa's face.

Use angle brush and Antique White to add mustache.

Use angle brush and Brown Velvet to shade outer edges of Santa's face and mustache.

Dip end of paintbrush handle into Rouge and add a small dot for nose.

Use flat brush and an up-and-down motion to add Antique White to trim of hat, allowing some of the Antique Gold to show through. When dry, add a bit of Brown Velvet to the trim of hat in the same way.

Use black marker to add a dashed line to the top and bottom edges of trim on hat. In same way, add a dashed line to outer edge of star.

Spray shoehorn with two coats of gloss sealer following manufacturer's instructions. Let dry.

Thread one end of fabric strip through hole in shoehorn. Tie ends together for hanger. Glue star to hanger. Let dry.

EACH KNIFE: Drill a hole through the top of the handle of the knife.

Use pencil to draw a narrow band along one side of top of blade for hat trim. In the same way, draw the outline of the face as shown in photo.

Use flat brush and Black Cherry to paint all sides of knife handle for hat.

Use flat brush and Antique Gold to paint narrow band along top of blade for hat trim.

Use flat brush and Fleshtone to paint Santa's face.

Use flat brush and Antique White to paint remainder of front of knife for beard. Also paint the tip of handle and the remainder of back of knife.

Use flat brush and Brown Velvet to shade outer edge of beard. With a nearly dry brush, add some vertical streaks to the beard.

Dip toothpick into Black and add two small dots for eyes.

Use liner and Antique White to add eyebrows.

Dip toothpick into Antique White and add a tiny dot to each eye for highlight.

Dip angle brush into Rouge and wipe off excess paint onto paper towel. With a nearly dry brush and a circular motion, add cheeks to Santa's face.

Use angle brush and Antique White to add mustache.

Use angle brush and Brown Velvet to shade outer edges of Santa's face and mustache.

Dip end of paintbrush handle into Rouge and add a small dot above mustache for nose.

Use flat brush and an up-and-down motion to add Antique White to trim of hat, allowing some of the Antique Gold to show through. When dry, add a bit of Brown Velvet to the trim of hat in the same way.

Spray knife with two coats of gloss sealer following manufacturer's instructions. Let dry.

Glue a garland piece to lower edge of handle. Let dry.

Thread one end of ribbon through hole in knife. Tie ends together to form hanger. ❈

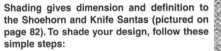

Helpful Painting Hints

Shading gives dimension and definition to the Shoehorn and Knife Santas (pictured on page 82). To shade your design, follow these simple steps:

1. Dip the paintbrush into clean water and gently touch the brush to a paper towel so the shine disappears. The brush should be wet but not dripping wet.

2. Dab the paint onto a foam plate or palette. (You could also dab it onto a disposable plastic plate, a plastic-coated paper plate, a glass plate, the lid from a disposable food container or a piece of plastic-coated freezer paper.) Touch a corner of your brush into the paint.

3. Stroke the brush on your plate or palette to blend the paint with the water so the color fades from dark to light to clear.

4. Position the paint-filled edge of the brush along the line or edge to be shaded and pull the brush along the line or edge.

Sweeten the Season With 'Frosty' Candy

TREAT kids to these fun figures from Helen Rafson of Louisville, Kentucky. "They look cute displayed together in a bowl," she notes. "With the candy canes, they can also hang on a tree."

MATERIALS NEEDED (for both):
Patterns on this page and page 85
Tracing paper and pencil
Water container
Paper towels
Foam plate or palette
Small flat paintbrush
Toothpick
Black fine-line permanent marker
Black florist wire
Craft glue
Ruler
Scissors
Two candy canes

MATERIALS NEEDED (for foam snowman):
3-1/2-inch x 4-inch piece of white craft foam
Acrylic craft paints—red and white
Pink card stock
1/4-inch heart-shape punch
5mm orange pom-pom
Two 4mm black half-balls or half-beads
Two 12mm green tinsel pom-poms
4-1/2-inch length of 3/8-inch-wide red-and-green stripe ribbon

MATERIALS NEEDED (for fabric snowman):
3-inch x 4-1/2-inch piece of dark green stiffened felt
Scrap of red print fabric
Scrap of white-on-white print fabric
Paper-backed fusible web
Acrylic craft paints—black, red and white
Two red 6mm pom-poms
Two 1/4-inch black buttons
White six-strand embroidery floss
Hand-sewing needle
3-1/4-inch length of 3/8-inch-wide red-and-green check ribbon
Masking tape

FINISHED SIZE: Excluding the candy canes, foam snowman measures about 2-3/4 inches wide x 3-3/4 inches high and fabric snowman measures about 2-1/2 inches wide x 3-1/4 inches high.

DIRECTIONS:
FOAM SNOWMAN: Trace pattern below onto tracing paper with pencil. Cut out following pattern outline.

Trace around the pattern onto craft foam. Cut out following the pattern outline. Cut slits where shown on pattern.

For painting, keep paper towels and a container of water handy to clean paintbrush. Place dabs of paint on foam plate or palette as needed.

Paint mittens red, adding coats as needed for complete coverage and letting paint dry after every application.

Use marker to add dashed line around outer edge of snowman and to add mouth as shown in photo above left.

Punch two hearts from pink card stock. Glue a heart to opposite ends of mouth. Let dry.

Dip toothpick into white paint and add a tiny dot to each heart. Let dry.

FOAM SNOWMAN
Trace 1—tracing paper
Cut 1—white craft foam

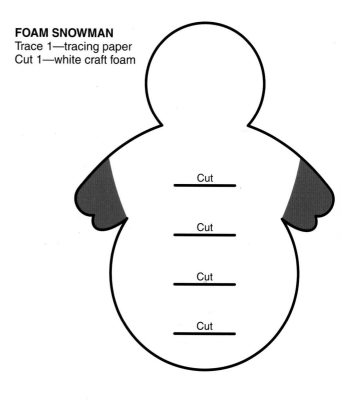

Glue orange pom-pom centered above mouth. Glue half-balls or half-beads above nose for eyes. Let dry.

Glue a green pom-pom to opposite sides of head.

Cut a 2-1/2-inch length of florist wire. Form wire into an arc. Glue ends of wire to back of pom-poms.

Tie a knot in center of ribbon. Cut ends in a "V" shape. Glue knot of ribbon to snowman's neck. Let dry.

Insert candy cane through slits in snowman.

FABRIC SNOWMAN: Trace outer snowman pattern onto tracing paper with pencil. Cut out shape following the pattern outline.

Trace around outer snowman pattern onto green felt. Cut out following pattern outline. Cut a 1/2-inch x 1-3/4-inch piece of green felt for candy cane holder.

Trace inner snowman pattern and each mitten shape separately onto paper side of fusible web, leaving at least 1/2 inch of space between shapes. Cut shapes apart, leaving a margin of paper around each. Following manufacturer's instructions, fuse shapes onto wrong side of white and red fabrics as shown on patterns. Let cool. Cut out following pattern outlines.

Using black marker, add dashed line around outer edge of fused white snowman shape and add mouth.

For painting, keep paper towels and a container of water handy to clean paintbrush. Place dabs of paint on foam plate or palette as needed.

Dip end of paintbrush handle into black paint and dab on two eyes. In the same way, add a small red dot to opposite ends of the snowman's mouth. Let dry.

Dip toothpick into white paint and add a tiny dot to each eye. Let dry.

Center and fuse white snowman onto green felt snowman. Fuse mittens to arms of white snowman.

Glue a pom-pom to opposite sides of head. Let dry.

FABRIC SNOWMAN

OUTER SNOWMAN
Trace 1—
tracing paper
Cut 1—green felt

INNER SNOWMAN AND MITTENS
Trace 1 each piece—paper-backed fusible web
Cut 1 inner snowman—fused white-on-white print
Cut 1 each mitten—fused red print

Cut a 2-1/2-inch length of florist wire. Form wire into an arc. Glue ends of wire to back of pom-poms. Let dry.

Separate white floss into three strands. Thread three strands onto needle. Stitch floss through holes in one button and tie ends in a knot on the front. Cut, leaving a tail of floss on the front of the button. Repeat with remaining button. Glue buttons to front of snowman. Let dry.

Tie a knot in center of ribbon. Cut ends in a "V" shape. Glue knot of ribbon to snowman's neck. Let dry.

Turn snowman over. Center candy cane vertically along back of snowman. Place green felt strip across candy cane. Glue ends of strip to snowman to keep candy cane in place. Cover ends of strip with tape. Let dry. Remove tape. ❄

Snowman and Bird Make a Merry Pair

A BIRD'S-EYE VIEW makes this frosty ornament extra fun. In Petaluma, California, Loretta Mateik used purchased wood shapes to form the whimsical snowman and feathered friend.

MATERIALS NEEDED:
1/16-inch-thick purchased wooden shapes (Loretta used Woodsies)—2-1/2-inch circle, 3-1/4-inch oval, 1-1/2-inch teardrop and 2-1/2-inch teardrop
1/8-inch-thick x 3/4-inch-high wooden bird shape
Drill with 1/32-inch bit
Water container
Paper towels
Foam plate or palette
Acrylic craft paints (Loretta used DecoArt Americana acrylic craft paints)—Antique Gold, Country Red, Evergreen, French Grey Blue, Hauser Medium Green, Lamp Black, Light Buttermilk, Rookwood Red and Tangelo Orange

(Continued on next page)

Paintbrushes—small flat and liner
Toothpick
Cotton swab
Textured snow medium
8-inch length of 1/16-inch-wide white ribbon for hanger
Wood or craft glue

FINISHED SIZE: Ornament measures about 4 inches wide x 4 inches high without hanging loop.

DIRECTIONS:
Drill a hole through the 2-1/2-inch wood circle piece, positioning hole near the edge.

Keep paper towels and a container of water handy to clean paintbrushes. Place small amounts of paint as needed onto foam plate or palette. Add coats of paint as needed for complete coverage. Let paint dry after every application. Refer to the photo on page 85 as a guide while painting as directed in the instructions that follow.

Use small flat brush to paint circle piece Light Buttermilk for head.

Use small flat brush to paint small teardrop piece Tangelo Orange for nose.

Use small flat brush to paint the large oval and remaining teardrop piece Hauser Medium Green for scarf.

Use small flat brush to paint bird Country Red.

Use small flat brush to shade the edges of the Light Buttermilk circle with French Grey Blue.

Use small flat brush to shade the edges of the nose with Rookwood Red.

Dip toothpick into Lamp Black and add two small dots to circle for eyes. In the same way, add a tiny dot to bird for eye.

Use liner and Lamp Black to add the eyebrows to the snowman and a curved line to the bird.

Dip cotton swab into Country Red and remove excess paint on paper towel. With a nearly dry cotton swab and a circular motion, add cheeks to the snowman.

Use liner and Antique Gold to paint the beak on the bird.

Use small flat brush and Antique Gold to paint the wide stripes on the oval scarf piece. In the same way, paint wide stripes on the large teardrop scarf piece.

Use liner and Rookwood Red to add narrow stripes to the center and sides of each Antique Gold stripe.

Use liner and Antique Gold to add dashed lines between the painted stripes.

Use small flat brush to shade the edges of the scarf pieces with Evergreen.

ASSEMBLY: Referring to photo for position, glue oval scarf piece to the bottom of the snowman's head. Glue the teardrop shape to the left side of the oval. Let dry.

Glue the nose piece to the snowman's head. Let dry.

Glue the bird to the tip of the nose. Let dry.

Thread the 8-inch piece of 1/16-inch-wide white ribbon through the drilled hole in snowman's head. Tie the ends of ribbon in a knot for the hanging loop.

Apply textured snow to tip of snowman's nose. Let dry. ❄

Mini Pillow Stuffs Season with Fun

ACCENT any plain space in your home with this cute holiday cushion. "I formed the wreath using the technique of needle punching," describes Mary Ayres of Boyce, Virginia. "It's easy to do and gives the design interesting dimension."

MATERIALS NEEDED:
Two 12-inch squares of white tightly woven fabric (Mary used weaver's cloth)
Ruler
Quilter's marking pen or pencil
DMC six-strand embroidery floss—three skeins of light blue and two skeins each of dark green and lime green
1 yard of dark green purchased piping for trim on pillow
12-inch length of 3/8-inch-wide coordinating ribbon
All-purpose thread to match piping and fabric
Polyester stuffing
Punch needle or needle punch tool and threader (see note)
6-inch embroidery hoop
Fabric glue
Standard sewing supplies

NOTE: Punch needle embroidery is worked through tightly woven fabric that is placed in an embroidery hoop. Loops of floss or thread are formed on the opposite side of the working surface to create the design.

A special tool with a hollow needle is needed to feed the embroidery floss or thread as the needle is punched through. Punch needle supplies are sold at most craft stores.

FINISHED SIZE: Pillow measures about 8 inches square.

DIRECTIONS:

Draw an 8-1/2-inch square centered on the wrong side of one 12-inch square of white fabric.

Place the fabric square wrong side up over the pattern at right so pattern is centered under fabric. Use quilter's marking pen or pencil to transfer pattern onto fabric.

With pattern centered, place fabric pattern side up in embroidery hoop.

GENERAL NEEDLE PUNCH DIRECTIONS: Use 30- to 40-inch-long lengths of embroidery floss for all punching.

If your needle punch tool has adjustable settings, set it so the needle tip is about 1/2 inch long.

Hold the tool perpendicular to the fabric. Work with the slanted edge of the tool facing the front or to the side, never to the back.

The floss that is coming out of the top of the hollow tube should be behind your hand. There should be no tension on the feeder floss.

Push (punch) the needle all the way through the fabric. Lift the needle out until the tip appears, then slide the tip a short distance and punch again. Check to see if the loops formed are the desired length. If needed, adjust the length of the needle to achieve desired loop length.

As you work, loops will appear on the underside of the fabric and a short running stitch will appear on the upper side.

Trim the tail of floss from the starting point after you have worked a few stitches, leaving about 1/8 inch of floss. Do not pull on the tail or you will remove your stitches.

When the end of the feeder floss reaches the top of the hollow tube, work a few more stitches. Then hold the last stitch in place with your finger. Lift the needle from the fabric and trim the tail of floss as before.

Add a drop of fabric glue to the ends of the floss to secure the ends.

Check the front of your work periodically to make sure your loops are the same height and are evenly spaced.

WREATH NEEDLE PUNCH: For all punching, separate six-strand floss and thread needle punch tool with three strands following the instructions that come with the tool.

Punch green outlines of wreath using dark green floss.

Fill in center of wreath with light blue floss.

Fill in light and dark green sections of wreath with dark green and lime green floss, alternating the colors as shown on the pattern.

Punch outline of square with light blue floss. Then fill in

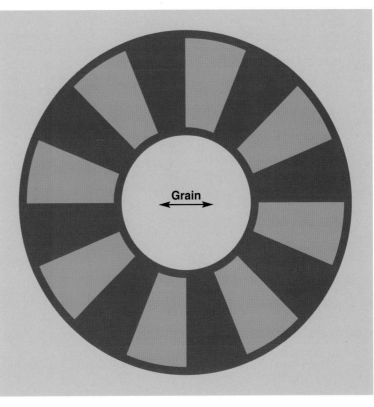

Grain

the background as shown.

Remove punched design from hoop.

ASSEMBLY: Trim away excess fabric on punched piece, cutting on the outline of the 8-1/2-inch square. Trim remaining 12-inch square to 8-1/2 inches.

Beginning and ending at a corner and with raw edges matching, sew piping to outside edges of punched piece with a 1/4-inch seam. Clip piping seam at each corner as you sew it to the fabric square.

Pin remaining 8-1/2-inch square of fabric to punched design with right sides facing.

Sew fabric squares together, stitching just inside previous stitching and leaving a 4-inch opening for turning. Trim corners diagonally.

Turn pillow right side out. Fill pillow with stuffing.

Turn raw edges of opening in and hand-sew opening closed.

FINISHING: Tie ribbon into a small bow. Hand-sew bow to top of wreath. ✿

Try a Sweet Variation

The simple needle-punch pattern on this pillow could easily be transformed from a holiday wreath into a peppermint candy disk. Just use alternating red and white embroidery floss for the sections of the wreath and use white embroidery floss for the center area of the wreath. For a different background color, try Christmas green, lime green or pale pink.

Adorable Angels Are Quick to Stitch

IF YOU enjoy cross-stitching but not time-consuming projects, you'll find these cheery cherubs divine. "Each stuffed ornament can be worked up in a few hours," notes Penny Duff from Kennebunk, Maine. "The first one was so fun to do, I just kept going!"

MATERIALS NEEDED (for all):
Charts on page 89
Twelve 4-inch square pieces of antique white 14-count Aida cloth
DMC six-strand embroidery floss in the colors listed on the color key
Size 24 tapestry needle
Polyester stuffing
Scissors

FINISHED SIZE: Excluding hanging loop, each ornament measures about 2-3/4 inches wide x 2-1/2 inches high. Cross-stitched design area of ornaments is 19 to 21 stitches wide x 22 stitches high and measures about 1-7/8 inches wide x 1-1/2 inches high.

DIRECTIONS:
Zigzag or overcast the edges of six pieces of Aida cloth to prevent fraying. To find the center of each, fold each overcast piece in half crosswise and then fold it in half lengthwise and mark where the folds intersect.

Draw lines across the charts, connecting opposite arrows. Mark where the lines intersect. Begin stitching here for a centered design.

Each square on the charts represents one set of fabric threads surrounded by four holes. Each stitch is worked over one set of threads with the needle passing through the holes.

The color and/or symbol inside each square on the chart, along with the color key, tells which color of six-strand embroidery floss to use to make cross-stitches and where to make gold metallic cross-stitches. Wide lines on the chart show where to make backstitches. Dashed lines show where to work running stitches. See Figs. 1-4 on page 89 for stitch illustrations.

Use 18-inch lengths of floss. Longer strands tend to tangle and fray. Separate the strands of floss and thread the needle with three strands for all cross-stitches except gold metallic. Use two strands for gold metallic cross-stitches and one strand for backstitches, French knots and running stitches.

To begin stitching, leave a 1-inch tail of floss on back of work and hold tail in place while working the first few stitches over it. To end stitching, run the needle under a few stitches in back before clipping the floss close to work.

When all stitching is complete, and only if necessary, gently wash the stitched pieces in lukewarm water. Press each right side down on a terry towel to dry.

ORNAMENT ASSEMBLY: Place a stitched piece of Aida cloth right side up on top of an unstitched piece of Aida cloth with the edges even.

Thread needle with unseparated white floss. Stitch the two pieces together, stitching through every other square two squares outside the red metallic running stitch and stuffing the ornament as you stitch.

Trim excess Aida cloth from assembled ornament, cutting through both layers five squares out from the white stitch-ing. Pull threads to create fringe, leaving one square on all sides remaining.

For hanging loop, thread needle with a 10-inch length of gold metallic floss. On the back of the ornament, stitch in and out of one square at each top corner. Remove needle and knot ends of metallic thread together. ❀

ORNAMENT CHARTS

ORNAMENT KEY	DMC
⊡ White	
▣ Medium Red	304
◪ Dark Pistachio Green	367
◩ Light Pistachio Green	368
▣ Light Hazelnut Brown	422
▪ Medium Brown	433
▢ Light Old Gold	676
◉ Medium Pink	776
▬ Medium Beige Brown	840
☒ Copper	921
◉ Dark Antique Blue	930
▣ Medium Antique Blue	931
◎ Light Antique Blue	932
▢ Light Tawny	951
▣ Medium Antique Violet	3041
▢ Light Antique Violet	3042
▨ Gold Metallic (2 strands)	5282
BACKSTITCH	
— Medium Red	304
▬ Very Dark Coffee Brown	898
— Gold Metallic (2 strands)	5282
FRENCH KNOT	
● Very Dark Coffee Brown	898
RUNNING STITCH	
-- Red Metallic	5270

Fig. 1 Cross-stitch

Fig. 2 Backstitch

Fig. 3 Running stitch

Fig. 4 French knot

Adorn Ornaments With Easy Crochet

FOR INSTANT ELEGANCE, *cover plain ball ornaments with these lacy crocheted pieces. In Elba, Alabama, Edith Calhoun created four patterns you'll love to play "dress up" with!*

MATERIALS NEEDED (for all):
Twilley's Goldfingering metallic yarn—one ball each of Multi-Goldfingering Golddigger metallic yarn, Purple Goldfingering metallic yarn, Silver Goldfingering metallic yarn and Teal Goldfingering metallic yarn (see shopping information)
Size 6 (1.75mm) steel crochet hook
Scissors
Assorted ball ornaments

SHOPPING INFORMATION: Twilley's Goldfingering metallic yarn is available from Herrschners. Call 1-800/441-0838 or visit *www.herrschners.com.*

FINISHED SIZE: Size will vary depending of size of ball ornaments. Gold ornament is about 2-3/4 inches in diameter. Purple ornament is about 3 inches in diameter. Silver ornament is about 2-1/2 inches in diameter. Teal ornament is about 1-3/4 inches in diameter.

DIRECTIONS:
GOLD ORNAMENT: With gold yarn, ch 8, join with a sl st in first ch made to form a ring.

Round 1: Ch 4 for first tr, work 2 trs in ring keeping last lp of each on hk, yo and draw yarn through all lps on hk to make a tr cl, ch 5, [work 3 tr cl in ring, ch 5] five times, join with a sl st in top of first tr cl: 6 tr cls.

Round 2: In each ch-sp around, work (1 sc, 1 hdc, 2 dcs, 1 hdc, 1 sc), join with a sl st in first sc.

Round 3: Ch 8 [sc between the next 2 dcs, ch 5, dc between the next 2 scs, ch 5] around, join with a sl st in the third ch of the beginning ch-8.

Round 4: Sl st in next ch-sp, sc in ch-sp, ch 3, sc in same sp, [ch 5, (sc in next ch-sp, ch 3, sc) in same sp] around, ch 2, dc in first sc to bring yarn up to start next round.

Round 5: Sc in same ch-sp, [ch 6, sc in next ch-sp] around, ch 3, dc in first sc.

Rounds 6-10: Repeat Round 5. Leave an 8-inch length of yarn at the end of last round. Thread end through ch-sps of last round made.

Slip cover over ornament. Pull yarn end to tighten cover around top of ornament. Fasten yarn and clip end.

PURPLE ORNAMENT: With purple yarn, ch 6, join with a sl st in first ch made to form a ring.

Round 1: Ch 3 for first dc, work 17 dcs in ring, join with a sl st in top of beginning ch 3: 18 dcs.

Round 2: Ch 8, [sk 1 dc, sc in next dc] around, ch 4, tr in last dc to bring yarn up to start next round.

Round 3: Sc in top of lp, ch 3, sc in same sp, [ch 6, sc in next ch-sp, ch 3, sc in same ch-sp] around, ch 3, dc in first sc.

Rounds 4-7: Repeat Round 3. Leave an 8-inch length of yarn at the end of last round. Thread end through ch-sps of last round made.

Slip cover over ornament. Pull yarn end to tighten cover around top of ornament. Fasten yarn and clip end.

SILVER ORNAMENT: With silver yarn, ch 6, join with a sl st in first ch made to form a ring.

Round 1: Ch 3 for first dc, dc in ring, [ch 2, work 2 dcs in ring] seven times, ch 2, join with a sl st in top of beginning ch-3.

Round 2: Sl st in next ch-2 sp, ch 3, work (1 dc, ch 2, 2 dcs) in same ch-sp, [in next ch-sp, work 1 dc, ch 2, 1 dc, in next ch-sp, work 2 dcs, ch 2, 2 dcs] around, join with a sl st in top of beginning ch-3.

Round 3: Sl st in next ch-2 sp, ch 5, dc in same ch-sp, ch 1, [in next ch-2 sp, work 2 dcs, ch 2, 2 dcs, ch 1, in next ch-2 sp, work 1 dc, ch 2, 1 dc, ch 1] around, join with a sl st in third ch of beginning ch-5.

Round 4: Sl st in next ch-2 sp, sc in same ch-sp, [ch 8, sc in next ch-2 sp] around to beginning ch-2 sp, ch 4, tr in first sc to bring yarn up to start next round.

Round 5: Sc in same sp, ch 3, sc in same sp, [ch 6, sc in next ch-sp, ch 3, sc in same sp] around, ch 3, dc in first sc.

Rounds 6-7: Sc in ch-sp [ch 6, sc in next ch-sp] around, ch 3, dc in first sc. Leave an 8-inch length of yarn at the end of last round. Thread end through ch-sps of last round made.

Slip cover over ornament. Pull yarn end to tighten cover around top of ornament. Fasten yarn and clip end.

TEAL ORNAMENT: With teal yarn, ch 6, join with a sl st in first ch made to form a ring.

Round 1: [Ch 8, sc in ring] six times. Ch 4, tr in ring to bring yarn up to start next round: 7 ch-sps.

Round 2: Sc in same sp, [ch 6, sc in next ch-8 sp] around, ch 3, dc in first sc.

Round 3: [Sc in ch-6 sp, ch 6] around, ch 3, dc in first sc.

Rounds 4-5: Repeat Round 3. Leave a 6-inch length of yarn at the end of last round. Thread end through ch-sps of last round made.

Slip cover over ornament. Pull yarn end to tighten cover around top of ornament. Fasten yarn and clip end. ❄

ABBREVIATIONS

ch(s)	chain(s)
cl	cluster
dc(s)	double crochet(s)
hdc(s)	half double crochet(s)
hk	hook
lp(s)	loop(s)
sc(s)	single crochet(s)
sl	slip
sk	skip
sp(s)	space(s)
st(s)	stitch(es)
tr(s)	treble crochet(s)
yo	yarn over
[ ]	Instructions between brackets are repeated as directed.
( )	Instructions between parentheses are all worked in stitch or space indicated.

Snowman Candle Lights Up Christmas

THIS FROSTY FELLOW can really stand the heat! The clay snowman shaped by Sandy Rollinger accents a plain candle holder. "I painted the molded pieces and applied textured snow for added interest," she relates from Apollo, Pennsylvania.

MATERIALS NEEDED:
Sculpey UltraLight oven-bake clay
Satin glaze (Sandy used Sculpey Satin Glaze)
Two 7mm black beads for eyes
Toothpick
Foil-lined baking tray
Toaster oven or standard oven
Metallic paints (Sandy used Jacquard Luminere paints)—
    Crimson 544, Pearlescent Emerald Green 572 and
    Pearlescent White 568)
Glue (Sandy used Beacon Adhesives Dazzle-Tac glue)
Water basin
Paper towels
Foam plate or palette
Acrylic craft paints—black, orange and yellow
Red dimensional craft paint
Paintbrushes—liner and small flat
Textured snow medium
Plastic knife or palette knife
4-inch-high flat-sided clear glass votive holder
Frosted glass finish (Sandy used Krylon White Frosted
    Glass Finish)
Cotton swab
Powdered cosmetic blush
Ruler
Tea light candle

FINISHED SIZE: Candle holder measures about 4 inches wide x 4 inches high.

DIRECTIONS:
FORMING CLAY SHAPES: Condition clay.

Roll a 3/4-inch ball for head. Place ball on foil-lined baking tray, flattening ball a bit.

Roll a 1-inch ball for body. Place body below head on baking tray, flattening body a bit more than the head.

Roll a 1-inch teardrop and press it on top of the snowman's head. Referring to photo above, shape teardrop as shown for snowman's hat.

Roll a 1-inch-long log and flatten it onto hat for cuff of hat. Use toothpick to make vertical indentations along cuff of hat.

Roll a 1/4-inch ball for tip of hat.

Roll a 1-inch teardrop for arm.

(Continued on next page)

Roll a 1/2-inch-long x 1/4-inch-thick rope for the candle. Press candle onto inside of arm. Press narrow end of arm onto body about 1/4 inch down from head. Press wide end of arm onto baking tray.

Roll a 1/4-inch teardrop for flame of candle. Press flame onto top of candle.

Roll a 2-inch-long x 3/8-inch-thick rope. Cut the rope into three sections for the scarf. Flatten each section. Use toothpick to make indentations on one end of two of the pieces for the fringe on the scarf. Press opposite ends of these two pieces onto the left side of the snowman's head. Press remaining scarf piece around the neck of the snowman.

Roll a narrow 1/2-inch-long cone for snowman's nose. Press wide end of cone onto snowman's head.

Use toothpick to press beads into snowman's head for eyes and to make an indentation for mouth.

Roll eight tiny teardrops for leaves. Press each teardrop flat. Use toothpick to make a center vein on each leaf. Place leaves on baking sheet.

Roll twelve 1/8-inch balls for berries. Arrange the berries on the baking sheet in groups of three.

Bake all clay pieces following manufacturer's instructions. Let cool.

PAINTING: Keep paper towels and a container of water handy to clean paintbrush. Place small amounts of paint as needed onto foam plate or palette. Add coats of paint as needed for complete coverage. Let paint dry after every application. Refer to photo on page 91 as a guide while painting as directed in the instructions that follow.

Use flat brush and Pearlescent White to paint snowman's head, body and arm.

Use flat brush and Crimson to paint snowman's hat, candle and berries.

Use flat brush and orange to paint candle flame and snowman's nose.

Use liner to add a bit of yellow to flame of candle.

Use flat brush and Pearlescent Emerald Green to paint scarf, ball for tip of hat and leaves.

Use liner and Pearlescent Emerald Green to add a plaid design to snowman's hat.

Use liner and black to paint indentation for mouth.

Use red dimensional paint to add stripes to scarf.

FINISHING: Spray the glass votive holder with two coats of frosted glass finish following manufacturer's instructions. Let dry.

Use plastic knife or palette knife to add textured snow medium to rim of votive holder. Let dry.

Glue two leaves and a berry group to each side of rim of votive holder.

Place votive holder on its side. Glue snowman to one side of votive holder. Glue ball to tip of hat. Let dry.

Apply satin glaze to all clay pieces following manufacturer's instructions. Let dry.

Use cotton swab to apply a small circle of cosmetic blush to snowman's cheek.

Place tea light inside votive holder. ❁

Enhance Napkins In Elegant Beading

IT'S A CINCH to create beautiful beaded napkin rings for your Christmastime table. Just follow these simple instructions from Nancy Valentine of Paupack, Pennsylvania.

MATERIALS NEEDED (for one napkin ring):
Fifty-six 3mm round gold beads
Twenty-eight 6mm round gold beads
Fourteen 8mm green faceted beads
Fourteen 4mm red faceted beads
30-inch length of 24-gauge green craft wire
1 yard of clear monofilament nylon cord
Needle-nose pliers

Wire cutters
Two large-eye hand-sewing needles (optional)

FINISHED SIZE: Napkin ring measures about 5/8 inch wide x 2 inches across.

DIRECTIONS:

ROW 1: Center one green faceted bead on the 30-inch length of green craft wire. Add a 6mm gold bead to the opposite ends of the wire.

Keeping beads centered, insert both ends of the wire through opposite sides of another green faceted bead. Pull the wire ends taut to draw the beads together, keeping the wire ends of equal length. See Fig. 1 below left.

Add another 6mm gold bead to each wire end. Cross the

Fig. 1
Starting
Row 1

ends of the wire through one 8mm green faceted bead the same as before.

Continue to add green and gold beads in the same way until the beaded strip is 14 center beads long. See Fig. 2 below.

Add two more 6mm gold beads (one on each wire end) and curl the beaded strip into a ring shape.

Thread one wire end through the first green bead and pull the ends tightly so all beads touch. See Fig. 3 at bottom left. Twist the wire ends together to secure. Use the wire cutters to clip the excess wire. Bend the twisted wire ends to the inside of the ring.

ROW 2: Thread one end of the clear nylon monofilament cord through any green bead of Row 1 and center the cord.

If desired, thread each end of the cord with a large-eye needle. Making sure the cord ends are of equal length, add a 3mm gold round bead to each end.

Insert both cord ends through opposite sides of a red bead. Pull the cords tightly to bring the beads close together.

Add another 3mm gold round bead to each end of the cord.

Insert the cord ends through the next green bead in Row 1 as before. Pull the cord ends tightly, making sure that the red bead comes to rest between two green beads in Row 1. See Fig. 4 at bottom right.

Continue to add beads in this way until beginning of row is reached.

Thread one end of monofilament cord through the first green bead and pull ends tightly so all beads touch. Knot the ends several times to secure. Use wire cutters to clip excess.

Shape as needed to form a ring. ❀

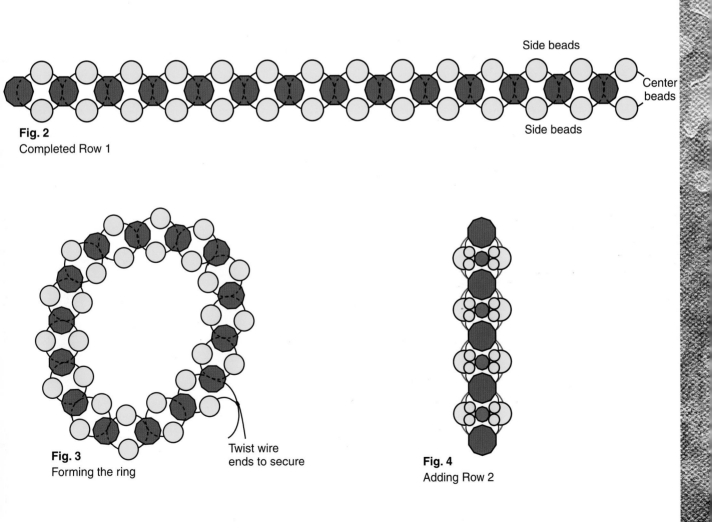

Fig. 2
Completed Row 1

Fig. 3
Forming the ring

Twist wire
ends to secure

Fig. 4
Adding Row 2

on back of canvas under completed stitches and clip close to work. See Figs. 1-4 at top of page 95 for stitch illustrations.

Using White Heavy Braid, fill in the cross with alternating Scotch stitches.

Using Green Heavy Braid, add the lazy daisy stitches.

Thread needle with a 20-inch length of 1/8-inch ribbon. To work the rose stitch, make stitches radiating from the same center hole for spokes. Bring needle up from the center and weave the ribbon over and under the spokes, keeping tension loose. Continue in this way until spokes are covered.

Overcast the outside edges with Christmas Heavy Braid.

FINISHING: Thread needle with 6-inch length of Christmas Heavy Braid. Stitch through top of cross from front to back and through the same hole to the front, leaving a loop of braid on the back of the cross. Remove the needle and tie the ends in a knot. Slip the folded end through the loop of ribbon near the knot. Pull to secure hanger and to position the knot at the back. ❁

Christmas Cross Has Joyful Spirit

GRACE your Christmas tree with this divine decoration from Susan Leinberger of Papillion, Nebraska. If you prefer, stitch a smaller cross using 14-count instead of 10-count plastic canvas.

MATERIALS NEEDED:
Chart at right
One sheet of 10-count white plastic canvas
Kreinik No. 32 Heavy Braid and 1/8-inch ribbon in colors listed on color key
Size 18 tapestry needle
Clear nail polish
Scissors

FINISHED SIZE: Cross measures about 4 inches wide x 5-3/8 inches high without hanging loop.

DIRECTIONS:
CUTTING: Remembering to count the bars and not the holes, cut plastic canvas piece as shown on the chart from 10-count plastic canvas.

STITCHING: Cut 18-inch lengths of braid unless directions say otherwise.

To keep the braid from raveling, dab a drop of clear nail polish onto the ends of each piece and let the nail polish dry before stitching.

To start, leave a 1-inch tail of braid on back of the plastic canvas and work the next few stitches over it. To end, run braid

COLOR AND STITCH KEY
ALTERNATING SCOTCH STITCH
🖊 Kreinik 100 White Heavy Braid
LAZY DAISY STITCH
🖊 Kreinik 008 Green Heavy Braid
ROSE STITCH
🖊 Kreinik 003 Red 1/8-inch Ribbon
OVERCAST/WHIPSTITCH
▬ Kreinik 238 Christmas Heavy Braid

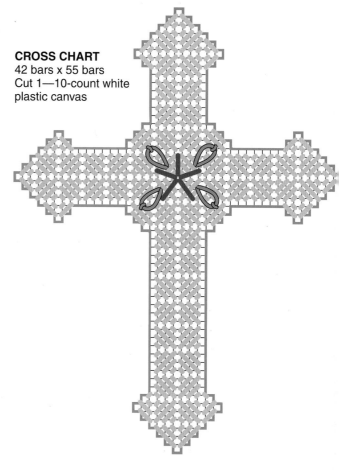

CROSS CHART
42 bars x 55 bars
Cut 1—10-count white plastic canvas

Fig. 1 Lazy Daisy Stitch

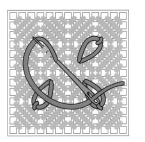

Fig. 2 Rose Stitch

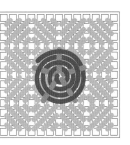

Fig. 3 Overcast/Whipstitch

Fig. 4 Alternating Scotch Stitch

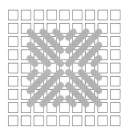

Wrap Up Fun with Simple Knit Scarf

FASHION this trendy accessory from Country Woman Craft Editor Jane Craig, and you'll have a wonderful Christmas gift for friends, teens…just about anyone! A ribbed pattern and metallic chenille yarn make this easy scarf eye-catching.

MATERIALS NEEDED:

Bulky weight yarn—three 1.76 ounce (46 yard) skeins of the desired color for scarf (Jane used Caron Glimmer yarn in Red)
Size 9 (5.5mm) knitting needles
Yarn or tapestry needle
Crochet hook (optional)
Measuring tape
Scissors

GAUGE: 12 sts and 23 rows = 4 inches. Slight variation in gauge will change the finished size a bit.

FINISHED SIZE: Scarf is about 5 inches wide x 74 inches long without fringe.

DIRECTIONS:

Cut thirty 12-inch lengths of yarn from one skein of yarn. Set yarn aside to use for fringe later.

Cast on 15 sts.

Row 1: K across row (RS): 15 sts.
Row 2: P across row (WS): 15 sts.
Rows 3-6: Repeat Rows 1 and 2: 15 sts.
Row 7: P across row (RS): 15 sts.
Row 8: K across row (WS): 15 sts.
Rows 9-12: Repeat Rows 7 and 8: 15 sts.

Repeat Rows 1-12 until all yarn is used or desired length is reached, ending with a Row 6 or 12.

FRINGE: Fold one 12-inch length of yarn in half. Use crochet hook or point of a knitting needle to pull fold of yarn piece through one stitch at a narrow end of scarf. Slip ends of yarn through loop and pull to tighten. Repeat, adding a total of 15 lengths to each narrow end of scarf. ❀

ABBREVIATIONS	
k	knit
p	purl
RS	right side
st(s)	stitch(es)
WS	wrong side

Cross-Stitched Trees Are 'Sew' Appealing

IF YOU like to sew or quilt, you'll love this set of creative Christmas trees from Ronda Bryce of North Augusta, South Carolina. Use them to decorate scrapbooks of your Christmas craft designs…or give them as gifts to crafty friends.

MATERIALS NEEDED (for each):
Chart on page 97
12-inch square piece of white 14-count Aida cloth
DMC six-strand embroidery floss in the colors listed on
  the color key
Size 24 tapestry needle
Fabric glue (optional)
5-inch x 7-inch picture mat in desired color (optional)
Scrapbook (optional)
Scissors

FINISHED SIZE: Quilting Christmas tree cross-stitched design area is 48 stitches wide x 78 stitches high and measures about 3-3/8 inches wide x 5-1/2 inches high.

Sewing Christmas tree cross-stitched design area is 52 stitches wide x 78 stitches high and measures about 3-5/8 inches wide x 5-1/2 inches high.

DIRECTIONS:
Zigzag or overcast the edges of the Aida cloth piece to prevent fraying. To find the center, fold the Aida cloth piece in half crosswise, then fold it in half lengthwise and mark where the folds intersect.

Draw lines across the chart, connecting opposite arrows. Mark where the lines intersect. Begin stitching here for a centered design.

Each square on the chart represents one set of fabric threads surrounded by four holes. Each stitch is worked over one set of threads with the needle passing through the holes.

The color and/or symbol inside each square on the chart, along with the color key, tells which color of six-strand embroidery floss to use to make cross-stitches. Wide lines on the chart show where to make backstitches. Dashed lines show where to make running stitches. See Figs. 1-3 below for stitch illustrations.

Use 18-inch lengths of floss. Longer strands tend to tangle and fray. Separate the strands of floss and thread the needle with two strands for all cross-stitches. Use one strand for backstitches and running stitches.

To begin stitching, leave a 1-inch tail of floss on back of work and hold tail in place while working the first few stitches over it. To end stitching, run needle under a few stitches on back before clipping the floss close to work.

When all stitching is complete, and only if necessary, gently wash the stitched piece in lukewarm water. Press right side down on a terry towel to dry.

FINISHING: If desired, center a picture mat over the stitched piece. Trim stitched piece as needed to fit on back of mat. Center and glue stitched piece and picture mat to the front of scrapbook. ❀

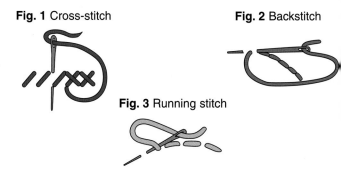

Fig. 1 Cross-stitch

Fig. 2 Backstitch

Fig. 3 Running stitch

QUILTING CHRISTMAS TREE
COLOR KEY

		DMC
☑	Very Light Moss Green	165
⊞	Very Light Jade	564
◼	Very Dark Olive Green	730
⊟	Very Light Yellow Green	772
⊠	Very Dark Hunter Green	895
◎	Medium Dark Rose	899
▨	Light Parrot Green	907
◼	Black Avocado Green	934
⊿	Very Light Dusty Rose	3716
◧	Dark Mocha Brown	3781
◆	Light Mocha Brown	3882
◙	Ultra Dark Beige Gray	3790
◩	Ultra Very Dark Turquoise	3808
◪	Dark Raspberry	3831
▣	Dark Bright Green	3850
⊡	Winter White	3865
▢	Metallic Gold	5282

BACKSTITCH
—	Black	310
—	Metallic Gold	5282

RUNNING STITCH
—	Dark Mocha Brown	3781

SEWING CHRISTMAS TREE
COLOR KEY

		DMC
☑	Ecru	
◼	Christmas Green	699
◼	Light Christmas Green	701
◉	Very Light Baby Blue	775
◼	Garnet	816
◎	Medium Dark Rose	899
◼	Dark Mocha Brown	3781
◆	Light Mocha Brown	3882
◼	Ultra Dark Beige Gray	3790
⊞	Dark Straw	3820
⊟	Light Straw	3822
⊡	Winter White	3865

BACKSTITCH
—	Black	310
—	Dark Mocha Brown	3781
—	Dark Straw	3820
—	Metallic Silver	5283

RUNNING STITCH
—	Dark Mocha Brown	3781

QUILTING CHRISTMAS TREE CHART

SEWING CHRISTMAS TREE CHART

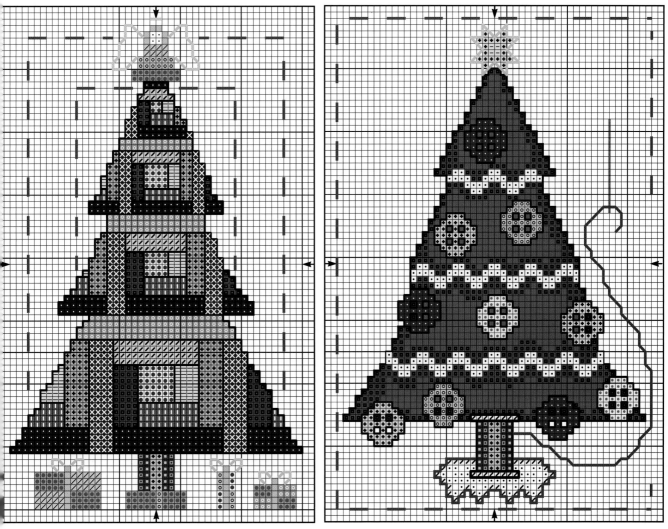

Paper-backed sew-through fusible web
Tear-away stabilizer
Buttons—four 5/8-inch coordinating two- or four-hole
   buttons and three 7/8-inch two- or four-hole buttons
Twig for hanging
Pinking shears
Standard sewing supplies

FINISHED SIZE: Excluding hanging tabs, wall hanging
measures about 8-3/4 inches wide x 19-1/2 inches long.

DIRECTIONS:

APPLIQUES: Use photocopier to enlarge patterns 200%, or
draw a 1-inch grid on tracing paper and draw patterns as
shown onto tracing paper. Trace three mittens and three
cuffs separately onto paper side of fusible web, reversing one
cuff and mitten for center mitten and leaving at least 1/2 inch
between shapes. Cut out shapes, leaving a margin of paper
around each.

   Following manufacturer's instructions, fuse mitten and cuff
shapes to wrong side of fabrics as directed on patterns. When
cool, cut out each following outlines of shapes.

   Fuse a mitten and cuff centered on right side of each 6-inch
background square with edges touching as shown in photo.

   Place stabilizer on the wrong side of each fused square. Applique each shape to background square with contrasting
thread and a blanket or satin stitch.

   Referring to photo for position, sew the three appliqued
squares together with a 1/4-inch seam.

   INNER BORDER: From small print fabric for inner
border, cut two 1-inch x 17-inch strips and two 1-inch x 6-
inch strips.

   Fold each strip in half lengthwise with wrong sides facing.

   Pin a 6-inch-long strip to the top and bottom edges of the
appliqued background. Sew inner border in place with a scant
1/4-inch seam. Do not press border out.

   In the same way, add the remaining inner border strips to
opposite sides of the background.

   OUTER BORDER: From dark print for outer border, cut
two 2-inch x 17-inch strips and two 2-inch x 9-inch strips.

   Sew a 17-inch-long strip to opposite long edges of the in-

Country Mitten Wall Decor Warms Hearts

*BUNDLE UP your decor with this appliqued accent. "I call the de-
sign 'Lost Mittens,'" says Mary Cain of Sun Prairie, Wisconsin.
"It seems at least one or two mittens disappear every winter!"*

MATERIALS NEEDED:

44-inch-wide 100% cotton fabrics—1/8 yard each of dark
   print for outer border and coordinating small print for
   inner border, 6-inch square each of three different light
   print fabrics for background, scraps of six different
   flannel fabrics for mittens and cuffs, and 1-inch square
   each of three different print fabrics for patches
10-inch x 22-inch piece of fabric for backing
All-purpose thread to match fabrics and contrasting color
   for outer edge of mittens
Pearl cotton or heavy thread—black or desired color for
   sewing on buttons
10-inch x 22-inch piece of lightweight quilt batting
Quilter's ruler
Quilter's marking pen or pencil
Rotary cutter and mat (optional)

**WALL HANGING
PATTERNS**

CUFF
Trace 1—tracing paper
Cut 3, reversing 1—three
different flannel fabrics

MITTEN
Trace 1—tracing paper
Cut 3, reversing 1—three
different flannel fabrics

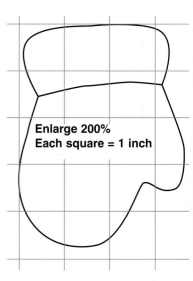

Enlarge 200%
Each square = 1 inch

ner border. Open and press seam toward outer border.

In the same way, sew the remaining outer border strips to the top and bottom edges.

QUILTING: Lay backing fabric wrong side up on a flat surface. Place batting on top of backing and center wall hanging right side up on top. Smooth out all wrinkles. Baste as needed to hold all layers together.

With thread to match background squares, straight-stitch around the outer edge of each mitten.

With matching thread, stitch in the ditch between the inner and outer borders.

With matching thread and a straight stitch, sew a wavy line in the center of the outer border.

FINISHING: Outer edges: Use quilter's ruler and quilter's marking pen or pencil to draw a line 1-1/2 inches out from each outer border seam. Use pinking shears to cut along each marked line, leaving a 1-1/2-inch-wide outer border.

Buttons: Use pearl cotton or heavy thread to hand-sew a 5/8-inch button to each corner of wall hanging.

Pin a 1-inch square of fabric to center of each mitten.

Use pearl cotton or heavy thread to hand-sew a 7/8-inch button to each fabric square, leaving long tails on the front. Tie tails in a knot on the front of each button.

Hanging tabs: From outer border fabric, cut two 2-inch x 4-inch strips. Fold each lengthwise with wrong sides facing to make a 1-inch-wide strip.

Fold each in half crosswise with raw narrow ends matching. Sew the raw narrow ends to top back of wall hanging, leaving about 1-1/4 inch of the tab extending above the top edge.

Insert twig into hanging tabs to hang. ❄

Make Tracks Toward This Polar Bear Pair

THE CUTE CUBS of the North Pole inspired Loretta Mateik to make some merry bears of her own. The Petaluma, California crafter created both a painted wood ornament for the tree and a paper topper for a holiday treat bag.

MATERIALS NEEDED (for bag topper):
Patterns on page 100
Tracing paper and pencil
Card stock—4-inch x 5-inch piece of white, 2-inch x 3-inch piece of gold and scrap of black
4-inch x 4-1/2-inch piece of dark blue snowflake print paper
Chalk—blue, brown and red
Black fine-line permanent marker
3-inch x 8-inch clear cellophane or plastic bag

2-inch length of 28-gauge gold craft wire
Stapler
Compass (for drawing the circle patterns)
1/8-inch circle paper punch
Craft glue
Scissors
Candy kisses

MATERIALS NEEDED (for ornament):
1/16-inch-thick purchased wooden shapes (Loretta used Woodsies)—one 2-1/2-inch circle for body, three 3/8-inch circles for ears and nose, one 3/4-inch circle for tail, one 1-1/4-inch circle for head, one 1-3/8-inch heart for legs, two 1-3/4-inch x 3/4-inch candy canes for front paws and one 1-1/4-inch star
Scroll or band saw
Drill with 1/32-inch bit
Water container

(Continued on next page)

Paper towels
Foam plate or palette
Acrylic craft paints (Loretta used DecoArt Americana
  paints)—Antique Gold, Country Red, French Grey
  Blue, Lamp Black, Light Buttermilk and Raw Sienna
Paintbrushes—small flat and liner
Cotton swab
One 8-inch length and one 1-inch length of 28-gauge gold
  craft wire
Wood or craft glue

FINISHED SIZE: Bag topper measures about 4 inches wide
x 6 inches high. Ornament measures about 3 inches wide x
4-3/4 inches high without hanging loop.

DIRECTIONS:
BAG TOPPER: Trace patterns below onto tracing paper. Use
compass and tracing paper to draw one circle each of the following sizes—2-1/2 inches, 1-1/4 inches, 3/4 inch, 1/2 inch and
3/8 inch. Cut out patterns. Cut 2-1/2 inch circle in half to make
a half-circle pattern.

Using patterns, cut out two paws, two legs, two 1/2-inch circles, one half-circle, one 1-1/4-inch circle and one 3/4-inch circle from white card stock. Cut out one 3/8-inch circle from
black card stock. Cut out star from gold card stock.

Lightly chalk all edges of each white shape with blue. In the
same way, chalk the edges of the gold star with brown.

Referring to photo on page 99, assemble bear as follows:

Glue the black 3/8-inch nose piece to the center of the
white 1-1/4-inch head piece.

Glue the 3/4-inch tail piece to the center top of the 2-1/2-
inch half-circle body piece.

Glue two 1/2-inch ear pieces to the top back of head.

Glue the legs to opposite sides of the head.

Glue the paws to the bottom back of the head so they overlap slightly at the bottom.

Use black marker to add two tiny dots for eyes. Also add
eyebrows, mouth and detail lines to ears and legs.

Use red chalk to add cheeks to head.

Use black marker to write "Polar Bear Kisses" on one side
of gold star.

ASSEMBLY: Use 1/8-inch paper punch to punch a hole
through the overlapped area of the paws. Use the same punch
to punch a hole through the top of the gold star.

Insert one end of the gold wire piece from back to front
through the hole in star. Coil end to hold wire in place. In the
same way, insert the opposite end of wire through the punched
holes in the paws and coil the wire as before.

Fill clear bag with chocolate kisses. Fold down top to
close bag. Staple as needed to secure.

Fold snowflake paper piece in half with right side out to
make a 2-1/4-inch x 4-inch piece.

Slip the folded paper over the top of closed bag. Staple in
the center to hold.

Referring to photo for position, glue assembled polar bear
right side up to snowflake paper, covering staple.

ORNAMENT: Use scroll or band saw to cut the 2-1/2-inch
circle and the heart shape in half. Set one half of the circle
aside for another project.

Drill a hole through one point of the star shape and through
the curved end of one candy cane shape.

Keep paper towels and a container of water handy to
clean paintbrushes. Place small amounts of paint as needed
onto foam plate or palette. Add coats of paint as needed for
complete coverage. Let paint dry after every application. Refer to photo on page 99 as a guide while painting as directed
in the instructions that follow. Use a small flat brush for all
painting unless the instructions say otherwise.

Paint one 3/8-inch circle Lamp Black for nose.

Paint the star Antique Gold.

Paint the remaining wood pieces Light Buttermilk.

Shade the edges of the Light Buttermilk pieces with
French Grey Blue.

Shade the edges of the star with Raw Sienna.

Dip toothpick into Lamp Black and add two small dots to
head for eyes.

Use liner and Lamp Black to add the eyebrows and mouth.

Use liner and Lamp Black to add the detail lines to the half-
heart shapes for legs. In same way, add details to the 3/8-inch
Light Buttermilk circles for ears.

Lay painted star flat with the hole at the top. Use liner
and Lamp Black to write "Joy" on one side of star.

Dip toothpick into Light Buttermilk and add a tiny dot to

BAG TOPPER PATTERNS
Trace patterns onto tracing paper and cut
out each as directed

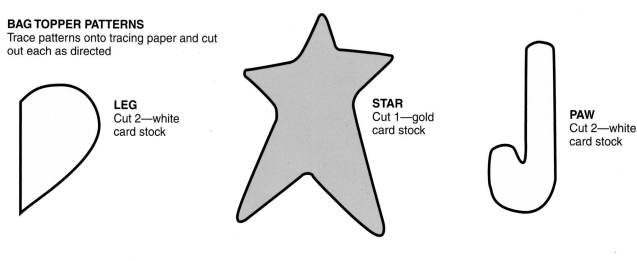

LEG
Cut 2—white
card stock

STAR
Cut 1—gold
card stock

PAW
Cut 2—white
card stock

each eye. In same way, add a small highlight to the nose.

Dip cotton swab into Country Red and remove excess paint on paper towel. With a nearly dry cotton swab and a circular motion, add cheeks to the head piece.

ASSEMBLY: Referring to photo for position, glue the tail piece centered on the back of the curved edge of the body piece. Let dry.

Glue the half-heart leg pieces along the lower edge of body piece. Let dry.

Glue the ear pieces to the back of the head piece. Let dry.

Glue the head piece to the body. Glue the nose to the center of the head piece. Let dry.

Glue the two paw pieces to the back of the body, overlapping them slightly.

Insert one end of the 1-inch gold wire piece from the back to the front through the hole in the star. Coil the end to hold wire in place. In same way, insert the opposite end through the hole in paw and coil the wire as before.

Insert remaining gold wire piece through the hole in top of tail piece. Twist ends together to form hanging loop. ✿

Fun Felted Handbag Makes a Stylish Gift

YOU'LL have Christmas gift-giving well in hand when you fashion this attractive tote from Country Woman Craft Editor Jane Craig. She began by crocheting a simple wool purse, then felted it and added purchased handles and beads.

MATERIALS NEEDED:
100% wool worsted-weight yarn (Jane used Patons Classic Merino Wool yarn—see note)—two 3.5-ounce skeins of New Denim
Size I/9 (5.5mm) crochet hook
Set of purse handles
Four silver beads (optional—Jane used Blue Moon Half-Circle Pendant silver beads)
Yarn needle
Scissors

NOTE: For successful felting, use 100% wool yarn. "Superwash" wool does not felt. Bleached white yarn does not felt as well as off-white and colored yarn.

GAUGE: Before felting, 15 scs and 15 rows = 4 inches. Slight variation in gauge will change the finished size a bit.

FINISHED SIZE: Purse measures about 10 inches wide x 9 inches high without handles.

DIRECTIONS:
BOTTOM: Row 1: Ch 46, sc in second ch from hk and in each remaining ch across, turn: 45 scs.

Rows 2-9: Ch 1, sc in each sc across, turn: 45 scs.

At the end of Row 9, work 8 scs evenly spaced across short end of piece. Work 45 scs along opposite side of beginning ch. Work 8 scs evenly spaced across remaining short end: 106 scs.

SIDES: Working in rounds, sc in front lp only of each sc around until purse measures about 12 inches from base, ending at one side of purse: 106 scs.

Sl st around top of purse to beginning sl st. Fasten off.

FELTING: To shrink and felt the crocheted piece, machine-wash piece in hot water using laundry detergent, running piece through a complete cycle that includes a cold rinse cycle. Without using detergent, repeat this process until piece measures about 10 inches wide x 9 inches high.

Smooth out wrinkles and lay felted piece on a flat surface to dry. Check piece while it is drying and shape as needed to maintain desired shape.

FINISHING: With matching yarn, hand-sew handles centered along top edges of front and back of purse.

With matching yarn, hand-sew beads just below handles on the front and back of purse. ✿

ABBREVIATIONS	
ch(s)	chain(s)
hk	hook
lp	loop
sc(s)	single crochet(s)
sl st	slip stitch

Scrappy Stocking Has 'Extra' Appeal

PIECE TOGETHER leftover fabric, and you can create this seasonal sock with time to spare. "I like that it works with a variety of different prints or solids," says Mary Ayres of Boyce, Virginia. "The boa at the top adds flair."

MATERIALS NEEDED:
Pattern on page 103
Tracing paper and pencil
44-inch-wide 100% cotton or cotton-blend fabrics—
   1/8 yard each of four different coordinating red prints
   and three different coordinating green prints
Two 12-inch x 20-inch pieces of white solid 100% cotton
   or cotton-blend fabric for lining
All-purpose thread to match fabrics
Quilter's ruler (optional)
Rotary cutter and mat (optional)
7-inch length of 5/8-inch-wide green grosgrain ribbon
14-inch length of white feather boa or feather trim
Fabric glue (optional)
Standard sewing supplies

FINISHED SIZE:
Stocking is about 10-1/2 inches wide x 17 inches long without hanging loop.

DIRECTIONS:
Either use photocopier to enlarge pattern 200% or draw a 1-inch grid on tracing paper and draw pattern as shown onto tracing paper with pencil. Cut out pattern.

CUTTING: Cut all strips crosswise from selvage to selvage.

From two red print fabrics, cut two 3-inch-wide x 7-1/2-inch-long strips for A and C.

From two green print fabrics, cut two 3-inch-wide x 7-1/2-inch-long strips for B and D.

From one remaining red print fabric, cut two 3-inch-wide x 9-1/2-inch-long strips for E.

From each remaining red and green print fabric, cut two 3-inch-wide x 11-1/2-inch-long strips for F and G.

PIECING: Do all piecing with matching thread, right sides of fabrics facing and an accurate 1/4-inch seam.

Referring to photo, sew strips A through G together for the front of the stocking. Repeat to make a mirror image for the back of the stocking.

Press all seams on front down and all seams on back up.

ASSEMBLY: Place a lining fabric piece on a flat surface with right side down. Place a pieced fabric piece on top of lining with right side up. Pin or baste around edges to hold the layers together. Repeat with remaining lining and pieced fabric pieces.

Place pieced fabric pieces together with right sides facing and with the strips and seams matching.

Pin pattern to layered fabrics with grain lines matching.

Sew sides and bottom of the stocking pieces together following outline of pattern. Remove pattern.

Trim away excess fabric, leaving a 1/4-inch seam allowance outside of stitching. Clip curves. Turn stocking right side out.

Turn 1/4-inch along top raw edge of stocking to wrong side for hem. With matching thread, stitch close to first fold.

Pin narrow ends of ribbon piece together for hanging loop. Pin raw edges to inside of back seam of stocking. Sew ends in place to secure hanging loop.

Glue or hand-sew feather boa or feather trim along top edge of stocking. ❀

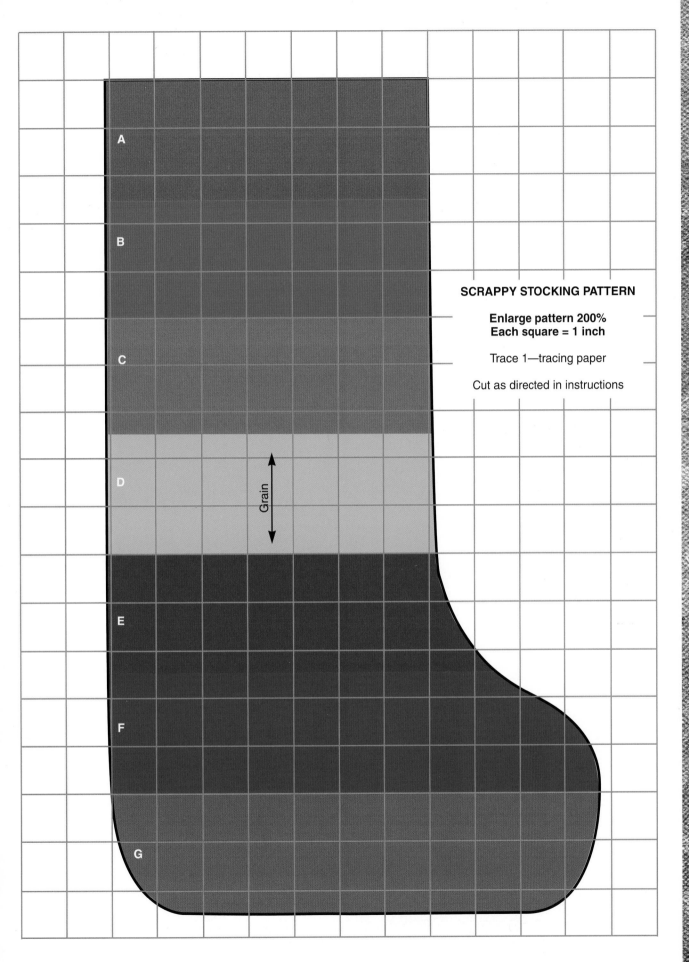

A

B

C

SCRAPPY STOCKING PATTERN

**Enlarge pattern 200%
Each square = 1 inch**

Trace 1—tracing paper

Cut as directed in instructions

D

Grain

E

F

G

Host a Christmas
Card-Making Party!

Easy card ideas, fast party foods and good friends... that's all you need to have card-making fun this holiday season.

WHAT A WAY to make merry during the holiday season—and to save money on Christmas cards at the same time! It's a party where guests make their own easy yet festive greeting cards, then enjoy a casual dinner of party-theme foods. Not only is this creative get-together lots of fun, it's fuss-free for the host, too.

In this special 8-page section, paper craft designer Jen Olski of Milwaukee, Wisconsin shares four of her super-easy card projects that make cheery Christmas greetings. Even a beginner can quickly assemble these surprisingly simple designs—from a beautiful stamped angel to a keepsake card featuring a holiday photo.

Plus, we've included a menu of scrumptious party foods (most of which can be made in advance), such as envelope-shaped sandwiches, a can't-stop-munching snack mix and cheesecake squares topped with pretty patterns. It's a complete meal that hungry guests are sure to love.

All in all, your card-making party will be a cut above the rest...and you'll find you can put it together in no time!

Here's How...

1. Invite five or so friends for an afternoon of card-making with a casual dinner to follow.
2. Gather the card-making supplies needed for the projects on pages 107-109. (Or, ask guests to bring their own papers and scissors while you supply the rubber stamps, ribbon and remaining items.)
3. Cover the card-making table in your home with a protective oil cloth or tablecloth.
4. Gather the ingredients for the party recipes on pages 110-111.
5. Do as much of the food preparation in advance as possible. (Check the menu at right to see which recipes can be made ahead.)

Paper craft designer Jen Olski (at right in photo at left) shows friends how easy it is to craft beautiful cards.

Menu

Paper Crafter's Punch

Bits and Pieces Munch Mix*

Layered Veggie Tortellini Salad*

Ham 'n' Swiss Envelopes

Patterned Cheesecake Squares*

Festive Fortune Cookies*

* = make-ahead recipe

Card Projects

Oh, Christmas Tree! Card

All Wrapped Up Card

Angelic Wishes Card

Joyful Memories Card

Jen's Tips for Making Cards By the Dozens

WITH a little planning and some doable designs, you can whip out dozens of stunning handmade cards in less than a day. Here are a few hints to help you get going:

Pick a design that you can quickly re-create.

Using lots of doodads and fancy paper-crafting techniques is great when you have to make only one or two cards. But when you'll be making dozens to send, keep it simple. The four card projects I've shared on the following pages are great ideas to start with. For more inspiration, scan crafting magazines or books...or flip through your holiday cards from past years for ideas.

Plan your project.

To make the most of your time—and your supplies—figure out how many cards you can create from your supplies. For example, from one 8-1/2-inch x 11-inch sheet of card stock, you can get two cards...or four layers for the front of a card.

Jot down a list of extra supplies you'll need so you only need to make one trip to the craft store. And be prepared to substitute if you run out! Remember that each friend and family member will receive only one card, so if theirs is a little different from the rest, it won't matter. In fact, it will be that much more special!

Work in steps.

Think of creating your cards as a one-person assembly line. Start by cutting your paper and trimming your ribbon so that every element is ready to go. Next, stamp all of your main

images. Then layer your main images, and finally, add your embellishments.

Your project will go much faster when you break it down into smaller steps. Plus, if you get called away, it's easier to pick up where you left off.

If you're traveling to a friend's home to make cards together, cut your paper before you leave. Or, just take along parts of the project that are easy to do while you're busy chatting or munching on snacks.

Add the finishing touches.

Don't forget about the inside of your cards! To save time, print out your favorite greetings from your computer using a coordinating colored ink, then trim the paper to fit the inside of your card. This works especially well when your card stock is dark and stamped inks would be hard to read.

Sign the backs of your cards with your name or initials and add the year. It's a personal touch that will help friends and family remember your thoughtfulness and the creativity you shared.

If you like, embellish the mailing envelope with a stamped image or greeting that coordinates with your card. The envelope will stand out in a pile of mail, and your recipient will know there's something extra special inside.

Oh, Christmas Tree! Card

SUPPLIES:
8-1/2-inch x 5-1/2-inch white card stock rectangle
4-1/4-inch x 4-1/4-inch x 3-inch green card stock triangle
1/2-inch x 1-inch brown card stock rectangle
1-foot length of gold cording
Buttons of assorted colors
Seed beads of assorted colors
4-inch length of 1/4-inch-wide ribbon
"Happy Holidays" stamp (Jen used Stampin' Up!)
Small star stamp (Jen used Stampin' Up!)
Red dye-based ink pad
Yellow dye-based ink pad
Double-sided tape or paper glue
Glue dots

DIRECTIONS:
Fold white card stock rectangle in half crosswise for card. On front of card, stamp "Happy Holidays" in red ink in upper right corner. With yellow ink, stamp star around words.

For the Christmas tree, fold green triangle in half width-wise. Crumple green triangle slightly. Unfold and set aside.

Thread beads on cord. Adhere one end of cord to top back of triangle. Wrap around to front, sliding beads to the front. Continue wrapping cord and spacing beads in the same way. At bottom back of tree, adhere cord. Trim off excess cord.

Wrap ribbon around brown rectangle and knot. Trim ends. Adhere brown rectangle to bottom back of tree.

Adhere tree to front of card, overlapping the stamped image if necessary. Adhere buttons to tree.

Jen's Project Pointers

• This card design is a great way to use up scraps of paper, card stock, ribbon and cording. Simply size the design to fit your scraps.
• Use leftover beads and buttons of different shapes and sizes for a more eclectic look.
• Get creative with color! Your Christmas tree can be any hue, and unusual background papers will create a fun, whimsical look for a holiday tree.

All Wrapped Up Card

SUPPLIES:
8-1/2-inch x 5-1/2-inch red card stock rectangle
3-3/4-inch x 5-inch green card stock rectangle
3-1/2-inch x 4-1/4-inch white card stock rectangle
"Merry Christmas" background stamp (Jen used DeNami Design)
Red dye-based ink pad
Green dye-based ink pad
Three 6-inch lengths of coordinating 1/2-inch-wide ribbon
Double-sided tape or paper glue
Glue dots

DIRECTIONS:
Place the background stamp on table with the image side up. Randomly ink background stamp with red ink pad, leaving uninked areas.

Using green ink pad, fill in the uninked areas of background stamp.

Lift background stamp and gently breathe on image side to moisten ink. Stamp image on the white card stock.

Adhere two lengths of ribbon to front of card, crossing the pieces, and adhere ends to back.

Center and adhere the stamped white card stock to the green card stock.

Fold red card stock rectangle in half crosswise for card. Center and adhere green card stock to front of card.

Tie remaining ribbon in a bow. Trim ends. Adhere bow to front of card where the two ribbon pieces intersect.

Jen's Project Pointers

• If you don't have a large background stamp, simply use individual word or small image stamps to fill in your white card stock. Think of it as creating your own gift wrap!
• Save time by stamping an entire sheet of white card stock with your background image, then cutting it to make the front piece for multiple cards.
• Instead of using two separate ink pads on your stamp, grab a multi-colored pad for a similar effect.

Angelic Wishes Card

SUPPLIES:
8-1/2-inch x 5-1/2-inch navy blue card stock rectangle
2-1/2-inch x 3-inch rectangle of white watercolor paper
1 foot of silver cording
Two blue beads
Angel stamp to fit size of white paper (Jen used Stampin' Up!)
Star background stamp or star wheel with handle and navy blue ink cartridge (Jen used Stampin' Up!)
Navy blue dye-based ink pad
Watercolor brush or blender pen
Glitter
Glue pen
Scissors
Double-sided tape or paper glue

DIRECTIONS:
Fold navy blue card stock rectangle in half crosswise for card. Using either a stamp wheel with handle and navy ink cartridge or a background stamp with navy stamp pad, stamp background pattern on front of card.

Use glue pen either to highlight portions of the stamped star background image or to randomly dot background. Sprinkle the glitter on the background and tap off excess. Let dry.

With navy ink, stamp angel on white watercolor paper. Using either a moistened watercolor brush or a blender pen, trace outline of stamped angel, carefully drawing out ink to create shadows and highlights or coloring in select areas of the image. Let dry.

String the beads on the silver cord. Wrap the cord twice around the front half of the folded navy card stock, positioning beads on the front of card. Secure ends of cord with adhesive on the front of card so that they will be covered by the stamped watercolor paper.

Using the blade of a scissors, distress the edges of the watercolor paper to create a frayed effect. Adhere paper to front of card, covering the ends of cord.

Jen's Project Pointers

- It's important to use a dye-based ink pad for the water-coloring technique. A permanent ink or pigment ink will not create the same effect.
- Any outlined image stamp will work beautifully with this watercolor technique. Just cut your paper to fit the size.
- For variety and visual appeal, set your main image off center on the front of the card.

Joyful Memories Card

SUPPLIES:

12-inch x 6-inch cream card stock rectangle
1-1/4-inch cream card stock square
2-inch cream card stock square
4-inch olive card stock square
2-1/2-inch olive card stock square
5-1/2-inch square of coordinating patterned background paper
6-inch x 1-inch strip of coordinating patterned background paper
6-inch length of narrow blue ribbon
1-3/4-inch oval punch
1-3/8-inch oval punch
1/8-inch circle punch
Small alphabet stamps or small "Joy" stamp (Jen used Stampin' Up!)
Small numeral stamps for year (Jen used Stampin' Up!)
Navy blue dye-based ink pad
Double-sided tape or paper glue
Photograph, trimmed to 3-3/4 inches square

DIRECTIONS:

Using navy ink and either alphabet stamps or small word stamp, stamp "Joy" along one edge of 1-1/4-inch cream card stock square. On 2-inch cream card stock square, stamp the year with numeral stamps.

Center small oval punch around stamped year and punch out. Use larger oval punch to punch out an oval from olive card stock. Center and adhere small oval to larger oval.

Punch an 1/8-inch hole on each end of the olive oval. Run the narrow blue ribbon through one hole on the olive oval to the back, bringing the ribbon up through the other hole. Set assembled piece aside.

Fold 12-inch x 6-inch cream card stock rectangle in half crosswise for card. Center and adhere large square of coordinating patterned background paper to front of card.

Center and adhere trimmed photo to front of large olive card stock square. Adhere bottom edge of stamped "Joy" square to the back of the upper right side of olive square so that the "Joy" piece resembles a tag.

Slightly angle assembled photo piece and adhere it to the coordinating patterned background paper on front of card.

Position the long strip of coordinating patterned background paper so that it covers the bottom edge of assembled photo piece and adhere.

Adhere assembled ribbon and oval piece to long strip of coordinating patterned background paper.

Jen's Project Pointers

- Lots of people create family scrapbook and memory albums. This Christmas card makes a perfect album addition after the holiday season.
- Select background papers to match your photo. In the sample shown at right, the olive card stock highlights the little girl's eyes (and her chocolate smudges!).
- Square cards will require additional postage when mailing. Check with your local post office before sending them. You could also easily adapt this photo design idea to fit a traditional rectangular card shape.

Paper Crafter's Punch

This tangy, Christmas-red blend will quench the thirst of any busy paper crafter. And with just four ingredients, it couldn't be easier to mix together. —Mildred Sherrer, Roanoke, Texas

    1 bottle (64 ounces) cranberry juice, chilled
    1 cup orange juice, chilled
    2 cups lemon-lime *or* club soda, chilled
Orange and lime slices

Divide the juices between two large pitchers; stir 1 cup soda into each. Add ice if desired and orange and lime slices. Serve immediately. **Yield:** 13-15 servings (2-1/2 quarts).

Bits and Pieces Munch Mix

You'll want to keep several bowls of this sweet-salty snack mix within easy reach during the festivities. Your friends will find it irresistible! —Marsha Beard, Shirley, Illinois

    3 cups popped popcorn
    3 cups Crispix
1/2 cup mixed nuts
    3 tablespoons butter
    3 tablespoons caramel apple dip

1. In a large bowl, combine the popcorn, cereal and nuts. In a small saucepan, combine butter and caramel dip; bring to a boil. Remove from the heat. Pour over popcorn mixture and toss to coat.

2. Transfer to a greased 15-in. x 10-in. x 1-in. baking pan. Bake at 250° for 45-60 minutes or until golden brown, stirring every 15 minutes. Cool completely. Store in an airtight container. **Yield:** 6 servings.

Layered Veggie Tortellini Salad

When you're finished layering paper to make Christmas cards, dig into this layered pasta salad. With a cheesy dressing, it's the perfect accompaniment to hot Ham 'n' Swiss Envelopes (recipe on page 111). —Dennis Vitale, New Preston, Connecticut

    1 package (16 ounces) frozen cheese tortellini
    2 cups fresh broccoli florets
    2 cups cherry tomatoes, quartered
    2 celery ribs, finely chopped
    1 can (2-1/4 ounces) sliced ripe olives, drained
    1 cup (4 ounces) shredded cheddar cheese
PARMESAN DRESSING:
    3/4 cup mayonnaise
    3 tablespoons grated Parmesan cheese
    2 tablespoons lemon juice
    2 tablespoons heavy whipping cream
    1 teaspoon dried thyme

1. Cook the tortellini according to the package directions; drain and rinse in cold water. In a large 2-1/2-qt. glass salad bowl, layer the tortellini, broccoli, tomatoes, celery, olives and shredded cheddar cheese.

2. In a small bowl, combine the dressing ingredients; spoon over the layered salad. Cover and refrigerate until serving. **Yield:** 10 servings.

Patterned Cheesecake Squares

With chocolate-sauce designs piped on top, these sensational squares will remind your friends of fun patterned papers from the craft store. And you'll love how easy these rich desserts are to assemble. —Laurene Hunsicker, Canton, Pennsylvania

    1 tube (16-1/2 ounces) refrigerated peanut butter cookie dough
    1 package (8 ounces) cream cheese, softened
1/4 cup sugar
    1 cup (8 ounces) sour cream
    1 egg
1/2 teaspoon vanilla extract
1-1/4 cups chocolate ice cream topping, *divided*

1. Cut cookie dough into 24 slices. Arrange side by side in an ungreased 13-in. x 9-in. x 2-in. baking pan; press together to close gaps. Bake at 350° for 12-14 minutes or until lightly browned.

2. Meanwhile, in a small mixing bowl, beat cream cheese and sugar. Add the sour cream, egg and vanilla; mix well. Spread 3/4 cup chocolate topping over warm crust. Carefully spread cream cheese mixture evenly over topping. Bake for 30-35 minutes or until a toothpick inserted near the center comes out clean. Cool on a wire rack. Cut into bars.

3. Place remaining chocolate topping in a heavy-duty resealable plastic bag; cut a small hole in a corner of bag. Pipe patterns on bars. Refrigerate until serving. **Yield:** 2 dozen.

Ham 'n' Swiss Envelopes

These clever envelopes may not hold Christmas cards, but your guests will still be eager to look inside. The hot pockets shaped with refrigerated dough are stuffed with a delicious ham-and-cheese filling. —Tammy Burgess, Loveland, Ohio

3/4 cup diced fully cooked ham
    4 teaspoons finely chopped onion
    1 teaspoon vegetable oil
3/4 cup shredded Swiss cheese
    1 package (3 ounces) cream cheese, cubed
    2 tubes (8 ounces *each*) refrigerated crescent rolls

1. In a large skillet, saute ham and onion in oil until onion is tender. Add cheeses; cook for 3-4 minutes or until melted. Remove from the heat; set aside.

2. Unroll crescent dough and separate into four rectangles; seal perforations. Place 2 tablespoons of ham mixture in the center of each rectangle. Starting with a short side, fold a third of the dough over filling. On the other short side, bring both corners together in the center to form a point. Fold over to resemble an envelope. Pinch seams to seal.

3. Place the envelope on an ungreased baking sheet. Bake at 400° for 10-12 minutes or until golden brown. Serve immediately. **Yield:** 4 servings.

Give Paper Crafters Fortune Cookies!

What could be more fun at a card-making party than fortune cookies, with their little paper messages tucked inside? You can easily dress up fortune cookies for Christmastime with this quick idea from the *Country Woman* Test Kitchen.

    Simply purchase a box of ready-made fortune cookies, plus red and green confectionery coating disks (such as Wilton Candy Melts). Melt the red and green disks separately in the microwave, then drizzle the colorful melted coatings onto the cookies and let them set before serving. They're festive, fuss-free...and yummy, too!

Our kids

YUM! Ask 3-1/2-year-old Marie Kathryn Prodell what she likes best about making Christmas cookies, and she'll likely say it's adding the sprinkles… and licking the frosting! Grandma Fay Prodell, Algoma, Wisconsin, sent the sweet photo.

GOD JUL…or "Merry Christmas" in Norwegian. It's the perfect seasonal greeting for cousins Dawson, Abbey, Carter, Eric and Lindsay Johnson, all dressed up in their sweaters from an aunt and uncle in Norway. Grandma Elaine Johnson of Torquay, Saskatchewan made the Christmas stockings.

I'VE BEEN GOOD! Santa is sure to deliver plenty of gifts for Carson Jeffrey Fisher. "He's our first grandchild and truly a little angel," says Norma Peterson, Wynyard, Saskatchewan.

FAMILY TRADITION. "Our 14 grandchildren perform our family's annual Christmas pageant," writes Fonda Masterson of El Dorado, Kansas. "Cute costumes and enthusiastic, unpredictable kids always make for a wonderful time."

SANTA BABY. Young Braxton got a kick out of his first Christmas, notes Grandmother Vickie Rodriguez of Graham, Washington. "Something was really funny to him," she relates. "He looked like he was laughing and dancing in his little Santa suit!"

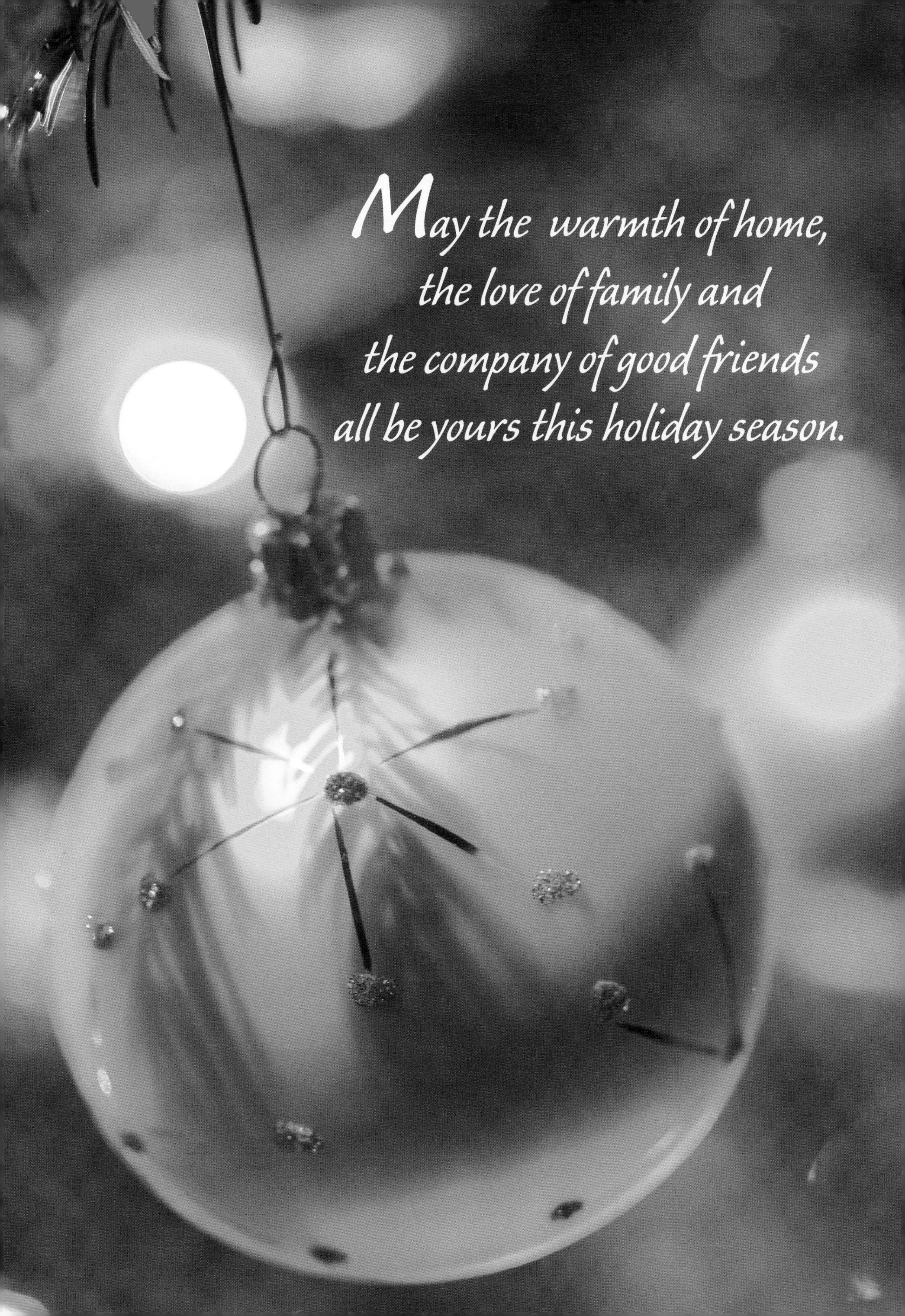

May the warmth of home,
the love of family and
the company of good friends
all be yours this holiday season.

★ Recipe and Craft Index ★

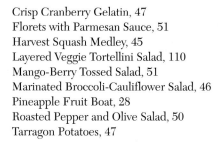